Limited Classical Reprint Library

THE EPISTLE TO PHILEMON

by

Samuel Cox

Foreword by
Dr. Cyril J. Barber

Klock & Klock Christian Publishers, Inc.
2527 Girard Avenue North
Minneapolis, Minnesota 55411

ISBN: 0-86524-134-1

Printed by Klock & Klock in the U.S.A.
1982 Reprint

FOREWORD

"The private letters of public men have a very special worth and interest to us. Of all documents, perhaps, these yield the most significant and accurate indices of character. In these we see the writer in undress, not in his robes of state; in his natural posture, not in any attitude struck to catch the general eye; as he was to his friends and intimates, not as he 'appeared to men'." With these words Dr. Samuel Cox introduces us to one of the most intimate letters of the Apostle Paul, and having done so, he proceeds to explain to us the true character of the writer.

Philemon lived in Colossae where he faced a difficult situation. The circumstances surrounding him were not unlike those faced by many in different parts of our country today. The city in which he lived was suffering from a severe economic "recession." The neighboring cities of Hierapolis and Laodicea were drawing away the trade. As if these problems were not enough, a cultic group spreading an incipient form of Gnosticism was seducing people away from the truth. Philemon was caught in the middle. He felt some responsibility to the citizens of the city as well as the Christians there. He was one of the leading businessmen of Colossae, and the church met in his house. Furthermore, his son Archippus served as the local pastor.

To such a man and at such a time the Apostle Paul wrote about a runaway slave.

It would be easy to dismiss the teaching of this letter to Philemon as being only a "tract for the times" with little or no relevance to us today. God, however, in His infinite wisdom saw fit to preserve this little piece of personal correspondence and include it in His Word. It is therefore worthy of our serious attention. Commentaries on the letter of Paul to Philemon are usually "tacked on" to detailed studies of Paul's letter to the Colossians. In this volume, however, two seperate discussions have been combined. They are Samuel Cox's remarks found in his rare work *The Private Letters of St. Paul and St. John* (1867) and A. H. Drysdale's *Epistle of St. Paul to Philemon* (1897).

Dr. Samuel Cox received his theological training at Stepney (now Regent's Park) College and London University. He excelled as an expositor, endearing himself to the people of his congregation, and was awarded an *honoris causa* Doctor of Divinity degree by the University of St. Andrews, Scotland.

Forced to relinquish his pastoral duties because of a loss of his voice coupled with a painful attack of neuralgia, Dr. Cox was compelled by necessity to make his living with his pen. He contributed articles to a variety of magazines including *The Nonconformist, The Church, The Christian Spectator,* and *The Quiver.* He also founded *The Expositor* and served as its editor for many years.

After several years of recuperation Dr. Cox so "regained the use of his voice as to be able to resume ministerial work. [His] power lay in the quiet, ardent study and exposition of God's Word, and he was not fitted by temperament, nor had he any inclination, for the noisy arguments of either political or religious controversy."

It was as a writer, however, that Dr. Cox made his greatest impact. His most famous works include his much sought after commentary *The Book of Ruth,* his study of Ecclesiastes which first appeared under the title *The Quest for the Chief Good,* and his extremely scarce *Private Letters of St. Paul and St. John*–a work of which Charles Haddon Spurgeon wrote:

> *Such exposition as this adds interest to the epistles, and makes their writers live again before our eyes. Mr. Cox delivered this work in public on certain week evenings. Happy are the people who are thus instructed.*

Samuel Cox's biographer records the satisfaction his literary accomplishments brought him. During his final illness many of Dr. Cox's friends wrote him. He remarked, "[my work] has won for me a friendly feeling in many thousands of hearts, which has been pleasantly proved by the letters which have poured in upon me from all parts of the English-speaking world. And it has procured for me a modest place among Biblical scholars to whom I am indebited for the most astonishing kindness, appreciation, and encouragement."

In this volume now before the reader, Dr. Cox's handling of Paul's letter to Philemon has been coupled with the devotional work of A. H. Drysdale (1837-1924).

Much less is known of Dr. Drysdale, except for the fact that he was an excellent student receiving both his M.A. and D.D. degrees from Edinburgh University. He served only three churches during his sixty-three years of ministry, the last of which spanned for more than four decades.

Dr. Drysdale wrote several books and numerous magazine and journal articles. His most popular work is his devotional commentary entitled *The Epistle of St. Paul to Philemon*–a study which appeared in the same series as W. H. Griffith Thomas' *Genesis: A Devotional Commentary* and F. B. Meyer's *Exodus.*

We are glad that these works are now available once more and commend them to a new reading audience.

Cyril J. Barber
Author, *The Minister's Library*

I.

ST. PAUL'S LETTER TO PHILEMON.

I.

THE EPISTLE TO PHILEMON.

PAUL, a prisoner of Jesus Christ, and Timotheus the brother, to Philemon our beloved friend and fellow-labourer,

2. And to our sister Appia, and to Archippus our fellow-soldier, and to the church in thy house:

3. Grace to you, and peace from God our Father, and from our Lord Jesus Christ.

4. I thank my God that I hear of thy love and of the faith which thou hast toward the Lord Jesus, and toward all the saints;

5. Always making mention of thee in my prayers,

6. That the fellowship of thy faith may become

Vers. 4—6. This sentence runs in a very involved form in the Greek, though its sense is clear. Literally rendered, it would read thus: (4) "I thank my God, always making mention of thee in my prayers, (5) hearing of thy love and of the faith which thou hast toward the Lord Jesus and unto all the saints, (6) in order that the fellowship (or the communion) of thy faith may become an energy in the full recognition of every good thing which is in us, unto (*i. e.*, to the honour of) Christ Jesus." As I read the verses, however, that for which the Apostle gives thanks is the faith and love which he hears that Philemon has evinced; and that for effectual in the full knowledge of every good thing which is in us, unto Christ Jesus.

7. For I have had much joy and consolation in thy love, because the hearts of the saints have been refreshed by thee, brother.

8. Wherefore, though I might be much bold to enjoin upon thee that which is befitting, yet, for love's sake, I rather beseech thee.

9. Being such an one,—as aged Paul, and now also a prisoner of Christ Jesus,

10. I beseech thee for my own child whom I have begotten in my bonds, for Onesimus,

which he prays is that Philemon's faith may grow into a completer fellowship with his own. To bring out this sense I have transposed the members of the sentence as in the text. I may also remark that it seems impossible, without a paraphrase, to give the force of the two Greek prepositions in the phrase, " the faith which thou hast *toward* the Lord Jesus and *toward* (or *unto*) all the saints." The meaning seems to be, that the faith for which the Apostle gives thanks is the faith which Philemon reposes in the Lord Jesus, and the existence of which he manifests and demonstrates by the kindly services he renders to the saints : the inference being, that faith in Christ, unless shown in works of neighbourly charity, is dead ; that kind deeds are the logical result and characteristic manifestation of faith in Jesus. And into what English preposition can one crowd so large a meaning as that?

Ver. 10. " *Being such an one :* " i. e., being one who is disposed to waive rights rather than to enforce them, who would rather entreat and persuade than exercise even an admitted authority, I do not command, as I might, but beseech thee, pleading my age and hapless estate as a prisoner, that you may be the more ready to relent and grant my prayer.

" *As aged Paul.*" What age was Paul when he wrote this letter ? It is impossible to determine ; all attempts to fix the date of his birth having failed. He may have been nearly sixty, he could hardly have been less, or much less, than fifty years of age : but though an ordinary man of fifty could hardly plead age, yet a man broken by so many labours, perils, sorrows, cares, as St. Paul, and exhausted by his fervid genius, may very well have been far older than his years.

11. Who was once unprofitable to thee, but now is profitable both to thee and to me,

12. Whom I send back. Do thou receive him that is as my own heart;

13. Whom I wished to have retained with me, that, in thy stead, he might minister unto me in the bonds of the gospel;

14. But without thy consent I would do nothing, that thy goodnes. should not be as by compulsion but voluntary.

15. For, peradventure, he departed from thee for a time to this very end, that thou mightest have him as thine own for ever;

16. No longer only as a slave, but as more than a slave, a brother beloved, very dear to me, but how much more to thee, both in the flesh and in the Lord.

17. If thou art in fellowship with me, welcome him as myself;

18. And if he hath wronged thee, or oweth thee aught, put that to my account—

19. I, Paul, write this with my own hand—I will repay it: for I care not to remind thee that thou owest me even thine own self.

20. Yea, brother, let me have profit of thee in the Lord: refresh my heart in Christ.

21. I write to thee relying on thy obedience, knowing that thou wilt do even more than I say.

22. But at the same time provide me a lodging,

for I hope that, through your prayers, I shall be given to you.

23. There salute thee Epaphras my fellow-prisoner in Christ Jesus;

24. Marcus, Aristarchus, Demas, Lucas, my fellow-labourers.

25. The grace of our Lord Jesus Christ be with your spirit.

The private letters of public men have a very special worth and interest for us. Of all documents, perhaps, these yield the most significant and accurate indices of character. In these we see the writer in undress, not in his robes of state; in his natural posture, not in any attitude struck to catch the general eye; as he was to his friends and

---

Ver. 23. *Epaphras* is mentioned first probably because, as he was a member of the Colossian Church (Col. iv. 12, 13), he would be the personal friend of Philemon.

Ver. 24. *Mark*, "the cousin of Barnabas" (Col. iv. 10), about whom there had once sprung up so sharp a contention between Barnabas and Paul (Acts xv. 36—39). *Aristarchus*, the Macedonian, who sailed with Paul in the "ship of Adramyttium" (Acts xxvii. 2), and who was now his "fellow-prisoner" (Col. iv. 10). *Demas*, who though now with the imprisoned Apostle, afterward forsook him, "having loved this present world" (2 Tim. iv. 10). *Lucas*, or Luke, "the beloved physician" (Col. iv. 14), and the Evangelist of the Gentiles, who, in all probability, was at this time the secretary or amanuensis of St. Paul.

intimates, not as he " appeared unto men." The
discovery of letters written in the abandon of familiar intercourse, and not meant to see the light, has
often changed, and sometimes reversed, the popular
estimate of men once thought to be very great or
very holy: while, on the other hand, the publication
of letters such as these has, at times, greatly raised
their author in the public esteem, his unstudied
friendly utterances disclosing a delicate grace and
beauty, or a largeness of mind and loftiness of aim,
or a devout tenderness of spirit, which he never
altogether succeeded in expressing while under the
eye of the world.

If, therefore, we had only St. Paul's public utterances, such, for instance, as his defence before King
Agrippa, or his magnificent oration on Mars' Hill,
or his pathetic farewell to the Elders of Ephesus,
or even the Epistles he addressed to the Churches ;
—if we had only these, although we should still be
able to form a tolerably large and accurate conception of the man, for more than most men St. Paul
wore his heart upon his sleeve, we should nevertheless lack some criteria, some indications and

"notes" of character, which it would be well that
we should have. For Paul, the Apostle of the
Gentiles, and, after the Lord Jesus, the greatest
teacher of truth the world has seen, naturally fills
a large space in the thoughts of Gentiles whose
"open eyes desire the truth." We think of him
much and often ; and it is of no slight importance
that we should form an accurate and complete conception of his character. And really it is hard to
say *what* that would really help us to such a conception has been withheld. We have, for the New
Testament, a singularly full biography of him by
St. Luke : nay, if we piece together the personal
allusions scattered through his Epistles, we have
an autobiography which covers all the essential
features and critical occasions of his life. We
have his speeches before kings and governors, and
before large public audiences, both of those who
believed in, and those who mocked at, Jesus and
the Resurrection. We have his Epistles to the
Churches, which expound his whole system of
thought, and disclose his method of instruction.
And, finally, we have the Letters he addressed

to private friends, such as Timothy, Titus,* and Philemon. There is no lack, therefore, of materials out of which to build up a true conception of the great Apostle, though I fear that many of his letters, letters which we should have been very glad to read, are irrecoverably lost. If we do not know the man, in his habit, as he lived, it is simply because we have not mastered his biography and autobiography, his speeches and sermons, his private Letters and public Epistles.

I.—Let us take up and examine one of these Letters,—the letter he wrote to his friend Philemon, about his friend Onesimus. Naturally, one of the first questions we ask about it is this : Does it correspond, in tone and spirit, with his public Epistles ? Does it reveal the very man whom we have so often heard teaching and preaching in the name of the Lord Jesus ? Or is there, as sometimes happens,

---

* The Epistles to Timothy and Titus, the *Pastoral* Epistles, can hardly be ranked as private letters ; for, though written to private friends, there is a breadth of tone about them which indicates that they were meant for a larger public than the friends to whom they were addressed, or than even the pastors of that time. Indeed, there are no letters in the New Testament which are strictly *private* letters, save the three discussed in this volume.

a wide difference between the private man and the
public character ?   I think we shall find that there
is no such difference.   I think we shall find that
the private letter shows us a man as courteous, as
large-minded, as ardent, as devout, as that Apostle
whose public labours and utterances have given us
so lofty a conception of both his character and his
genius.   But before we can answer this question to
advantage, we must a little consider under what
conditions this Letter was written ; we must also
learn what we can of the two men, Onesimus and
Philemon, whom it chiefly concerned.

When he wrote this Letter, St. PAUL was a
prisoner in imperial Rome—it contains at least three
allusions to his *bonds*—awaiting the sentence of the
Emperor Nero.   He had appealed to Cæsar, claiming his right as a Roman citizen ; and to Cæsar he
was sent.   In Rome he had to suffer the torture of
" the law's delay."   The official documents connected with his case had probably been lost in the
shipwreck off Malta ; it would be long before
duplicates could be obtained.   The prosecutors and

witnesses had to be brought from Syria to Italy, a
tedious and perilous journey. Nero was full of
caprice, and so averse to business that it was only
at rare intervals he could be got to hear a suit and
give his verdict. For these and the like reasons,
the trial of Paul was postponed for two years.
During this interval, through the humanity of the
Prætorian Prefect Burrhus, St. Paul, as Luke tells
us,* was allowed to dwell in " his own hired
house." But we must not suffer St. Luke's phrase
to mislead our thoughts. This " hired house " was
by no means the comfortable residence one might
suppose it to have been. The stately marble palace
of the Emperor, like the other patrician mansions of
Rome, was surrounded by wooden huts and cabins
tenanted by the innumerable train of slaves, minions,
and freedmen who were retained for the service of
the palace and its inmates. And it was in one of
these miserable dens that the Apostle was permitted
to reside, instead of being cast into the vast horrible
dungeons beneath the palace floor. Night and day,
moreover, he was chained to soldier after soldier of

* Acts xxviii. 30.

the Imperial guard, no moment of privacy allowed him ; and was, no doubt, often treated with insolence, if not with violence, by the rude mercenaries. With his right wrist chained to the soldier's left wrist, he sat for " two whole years " in his wooden hut, teaching all who came to him, and winning some of his guards, nay, even some of the minions and parasites of the Court—for he speaks of his successes in the Prætorium*—to the faith of Christ. " The care of all the churches " was upon him : messengers were constantly arriving and departing

---

* The Epistle to the Philippians, like that to Philemon, was written during St. Paul's Roman imprisonment. And in this Epistle (Phil. i. 12, 13), he assures his friends at Philippi that his " circumstances have fallen out unto the furtherance of the Gospel; so that my bonds have become manifest in Christ *in the whole Prætorium,* and to all the rest." The meaning of the phrase, " in the whole Prætorium," is disputed. It may mean either the palace of the Emperor, or the barrack (or camp) of the Prætorian guards. If we must choose between the two, I should prefer the former interpretation, since (Phil. iv. 22), the Apostle closes the Epistle with a salutation from " *they that are of Cæsar's household* " to their brethren at Philippi ; and thus proves that he had converts in the palace. But, to a certain extent at least, the two interpretations may be reconciled. For the Prætorians furnished the body-guard to the Emperor ; this body-guard had a barrack in the precincts of the palace, as well as a camp outside the city. And it was, probably, in one of the huts composing, or connected with, this barrack, that St. Paul was confined. Both barrack and palace were called the Prætorium ; and therefore when Paul speaks of his success in " *the whole* Prætorium," it seems best to understand him as affirming that in both the places which bore this name, in the palace and in the barrack, among the guards and among the retainers of the court, he had found willing hearers of the Gospel of our redemption. Merivale has a good note on this point in his " History of the Romans under the Empire," vol. vi. chap. liv. p. 438.

with messages, or gifts, or letters : and in the intervals of worship and teaching, the fettered Apostle dictated the Epistles he could no longer write, only adding a few words (as in Philemon, ver. 19) with his own hand—a hand so weighted and cramped with the pendant chain that his words were of necessity few, and the letters* he formed with it of necessity "large."

What a picture rises in the mind as one tries to conceive the scene ! There, in his wooden cabin, often "crowded" by anxious hearers of the Word, sits a scholar and a gentleman, exhausted by the labours of the day. The lamp shines down on his bald forehead, lights up the keen aquiline features of his oval face, shaded with grey hair,† and glitters from

---

* St. Paul, however, seems always to have written a bold dashing hand. Thus, for instance, writing to the Galatians (chap. vi. 11), he says, "Look ye in what *large letters* I write with mine own hand." The fact has been variously accounted for. Some attribute it to his defective eyesight, others to a nervous palsy, induced by his many sufferings, and especially by his long endurance of chains. Both these causes may have had something to do with the "large" handwriting of the Apostle ; but surely Theodore of Mopsuestia comes nearer the mark when he attributes "the boldness of the handwriting to the force of the Apostle's convictions." It was, in all probability, the bold fervent character of the man, even more than any bodily defect, which led him to use "large letters."

† This is no fancy portrait, or, if it be, I am not responsible for it. In all works of early Christian art, and notably in the Roman catacombs, St. Paul is portrayed as of short stature, bald head, bushy eyebrows, pointed beard, clear grey eyes, aquiline nose, and a long oval face.

the armour of the brawny Prætorian who lounges beside him, and from the links of the chain which binds them wrist to wrist.   Paul dictates sentence after sentence to Luke, the learned physician, who carries his pen and inkhorn at his waist.   He is inditing a letter to his friend Philemon in far-away Phrygian Colossæ, about a runaway slave, pleading for the outcast, promising that if in anything the slave has wronged his master, he, Paul, will be answerable for it.   The thought strikes him that the promise will carry more weight with it if written by his own hand.   He interrupts the flow of speech; cries, " Here, Luke, give me the reed!" and with benumbed labouring fingers inscribes these words, "I, Paul, write this *with my own hand*—I will repay it."

It is touching—is it not, to think of so great a man in such miserable conditions ?   A man so like the Master whom he serves that, while he carries whole races and churches on his heart, he yet has a special love for every wretched outcast who will accept his love; and is not only bent on serving him, but will take thought how he may best serve him, and spare no pains to make his service effectual.

PHILEMON, to whom St. Paul wrote, was probably a native of Colossæ, certainly an inhabitant of that Phrygian city. We know nothing of him save that which we learn from the hints given in this Epistle, as interpreted by the customs and conditions of his time. From these we infer that he was a large householder, a man of property and influence, addicted to hospitality, charitable to the poor, and that he had "a church" in his house, *i.e.*, gathered his brethren and sisters in Christ together for worship, and for the "feasts" which then accompanied worship. "The sister Appia," mentioned in ver. 2, was probably, as the early Greek commentators affirm, the wife of Philemon. "Archippus, our fellow-soldier," was a minister of the Gospel at Colossæ; for, in his Epistle to the Colossians,* St. Paul writes, "Say to Archippus, take heed to the ministry which thou receivedst in the Lord, that thou fulfil it." Probably too, as the commentators suppose, he was the son of Philemon and Appia, and the minister of the church in their

---

* Colossians iv. 17. It is not improbable, as some of the commentators infer from the warning yet inspiriting tone of this message, that Archippus was a young man *recently* called to the ministry of the Word.

house. These conjectures and traditions are, at least, so far confirmed by St. Paul's letter as this: that, in writing on a matter so strictly private as the conversion and return of a runaway slave, it is not at all likely that the Apostle would send special greeting to any but Philemon and the members of his family.

This Colossian householder had received the Gospel from the lips of St. Paul himself: for Paul reminds him (ver. 19) that he owed " even his own self," his own soul, to him; that is, he had been converted under the Apostle's ministry.* The good seed fell into a good soil: for Philemon became full of the faith which worketh by love (ver. 4); the hearts of many of the saints were " refreshed" by his good deeds and kindly help (ver. 7). Hospitable and charitable, he was also docile, only

---

* This conclusion has been questioned on the ground that St. Paul never was at Colossæ, that the Church there was founded by Epaphras, not by the Apostle. But in an age of commerce and travel, St. Paul must have preached to many men whose cities he never entered. A man of Philemon's position must, in all probability, have been often carried by his affairs from the Phrygian table-lands, on which Colossæ stood, along the great road from the Euphrates to Ephesus, which swept close by Colossæ, to Ephesus the chief port and market of the province. St. Paul taught three years at Ephesus. Is it altogether incredible that Philemon should have visited the neighbouring city during that time, and there have heard the good tidings of salvation from the Apostle's lips?

needing a hint of duty to go beyond the mere claims of duty. "I know," cries Paul, "that thou wilt do even more than I say" (ver. 21).

We may conceive of Philemon, therefore, as one of those Asiatic "lords," or "householders," to whom the Lord Jesus often refers in His parables; as having many slaves to whom he entrusted his goods, according to their several ability to use them; as a *Christian* householder, with a Christian wife, and a son a Christian minister, and a Christian church in his house; as a man of singularly *high* Christian character, full of love and faith and good works.*

Among his slaves was a certain ONESIMUS, a Phrygian by race, a Colossian by birth. In a Christian household, such as that of Philemon, we may be tolerably sure that slavery took its least offensive form; that the rule of the lord, or house-

---

* Tradition adds to all we know of Philemon, that he was bishop of Colossæ or of Gaza—which is very unlikely—and became a martyr at Rome during the persecution of Nero—which may be true, as also it may not. Theodoret says that his house was still shown in Colossæ in the fifth century after Christ; but I believe that to this very day they profess to show you in Jerusalem the house of that rich man at whose gate lay beggar Lazarus, and possibly the former relic was as genuine, *i.e.* as spurious, as is the latter.

holder, was lenient and gracious ; that Onesimus, in common with his fellows, would be fairly treated, and must have had many opportunities of hearing the truth as it is in Jesus. But something in the man, whether a virtue or a vice of blood, revolted from his condition, and rendered him impervious to the hopes and consolations of his master's faith. That Onesimus was a man of good natural ability and disposition seems evident from St. Paul's high appreciation of him : for Paul was no mean judge of men, and he loved Onesimus "as his own heart" (ver. 12); had found his company very "profitable" (ver. 11); and would have liked to retain him as a friend and minister (ver. 13). But, on the other hand, Onesimus was not a prisoner of war ; not, therefore, one of those most miserable of men who, more refined and of a higher spirit and culture than their masters, were, nevertheless, compelled to endure whatever degradation, or insult, or torture they were pleased to inflict upon them. He was a Colossian in the service of a Colossian.*

---

* In the Epistle to the Colossians (iv. 9), St. Paul speaks of Onesimus as " our faithful and beloved brother, *who is one of you*," *i.e.*, who is of

Probably, therefore, he was a home-born slave, with slaves for his parents, or a man of low class or habits who sold himself into bondage that he might eat bread. I am afraid, too, that Onesimus was a thief. For though it is possible to suppose that the wrong he had done his master was simply that of absconding from his service, yet the allusion in this Letter to the fact that Onesimus was once " unprofitable" to his master (ver. 11); the request, " if he hath wronged thee, or oweth thee aught, put that to my account" (ver. 18); and the promise, " I will repay it" (ver. 19), all seem to point to an embezzlement : they indicate that, allured by the prospect of liberty, and the chance of carrying off a sum which would make his liberty bearable, if not pleasant, Onesimus absconded with money or goods which his master had entrusted to him.

After many wanderings and perils, he arrived in Rome—the crowded metropolis, then as now, being the resort in which all fugitives from law or justice found their best chance of concealment. We can

your race and city, and not simply a member of your Church. So, at least, the best commentators read the phrase.

imagine with what a rabble of criminals, rogues, sharpers, gladiators, and fugitive slaves, Onesimus must have herded in the vile haunts of the imperial city, and how quickly he would squander his booty among them, or be swindled out of it. But, at last, a gracious Providence brought him to St. Paul's hut. Among " the crowd which pressed" on the Apostle " daily," there one day stood the Phrygian slave. His crime, or its evil punitive results, have awakened conscience; the cleansing healing truth comes home to him. As he listens, he repents, converts, and is saved. He tells his story to the Apostle, is taught his sin, and yet comforted with hopes brighter than he had ever known. He devotes himself to the service of the teacher of whom he had learned the way of truth and peace. Paul loves him—loves him so well that he can part with him for his good. He thinks it will be good for Onesimus to go back to his master and atone his trespass. He sends him back with Tychicus, who carries the Epistle to the Colossian Church, while Onesimus bears a letter to Philemon, the Colossian householder,—a letter which, I suppose, Paul

thought would never be read except by his friend
Philemon, Appia his sister, and his comrade
Archippus, but which the Holy Ghost has graciously
put into our hands.*

Here, then, we may return to the question with
which we started. We may once more ask, Does
this private letter correspond, in tone and spirit,
with St. Paul's public Epistles? for now we are in
a position to reply. We are able to compare the
Letter in the hands of Onesimus with the Epistle in
the hands of Tychicus—they lie side by side between the covers of the same Book—and to determine whether or not the Apostle is one man in
public, and in private another man.

Look at these two Letters, then, and you will see
that even in external form there is a close resemblance
between them. The Epistle to the Colossians opens
with the salutation, " Paul, an Apostle of Jesus
Christ by the will of God, and Timotheus the bro-

---

* To all we know of Onesimus, tradition adds that he became Bishop
of Berea, in Macedonia;—curiously enough, hardly a person is mentioned
in the New Testament whom ecclesiastical history does *not* make a bishop,
or a martyr, or both,—and died in Rome, a martyr to the faith.

ther, to the holy and faithful brethren in Christ at
Colossæ : Grace to you, and peace from God our
Father and the Lord Jesus Christ " (vers. 1, 2). The
Letter to Philemon opens with " Paul, a prisoner of
Jesus Christ, and Timotheus the brother, to Philemon our beloved friend and fellow-labourer : grace
to you, and peace from God our Father and the
Lord Jesus Christ " (vers. 1, 3). In the Epistle
to the Colossians, the salutation is followed by a
thanksgiving, " We give thanks to God, the Father
of our Lord Jesus Christ . . . having heard of your
faith in Christ Jesus, and of *the love which ye have
toward all the saints*" (vers. 3, 4) ; the thanksgiving is followed by a prayer, " We do not cease
to pray for you, and to make our petition that ye
may be *filled with the knowledge* of His will in all
spiritual wisdom and understanding " (ver. 9).
And in the Letter to Philemon, the salutation is also
followed by a thanksgiving for the very same graces,
" I thank my God that I hear of thy *love*, and of
thy faith which thou hast *toward the Lord Jesus*
and *toward all the saints*" (ver. 4.) : and the thanksgiving is also followed by a prayer for the very same

blessing, " Making mention of thee always in my prayers, that the fellowship of thy faith may become effectual in *the full knowledge* of every good thing" (vers. 5, 6). * In both Epistles there are allusions to St. Paul's bonds, and his chain is lifted in pathetic appeal ; † both close with greetings from the same saints,‡ and with an Apostolic benediction.§

Beneath this similarity of form there lies unity of spirit. Not only in his Epistle to the Colossians, but in all his public appearances and utterances, St. Paul was distinguished by a singular tact and courtesy. He carried himself like a gentleman versed in the best manners of his time, and of all time. This courtesy is very conspicuous in his letter to Philemon, so conspicuous and pervading, indeed, that it was commonly known to our fathers as " the Polite Epistle." For eighteen centuries, by men of all races and schools of thought, it has been admired as a model of composition, unsurpassed, and

---

* The reader, carefully comparing these citations, will discover many minute correspondences of phrase and structure which it was well nigh impossible to bring out in a spoken discourse.

† Compare Col. i. 24, iv. 3, 4, 10, and 18, with Philemon 1, 9, 10, 23.

‡ Compare Col. iv. 10—14, with Phil. 23, 24.

§ Compare Col. iv. 18, with Phil. 25.

well-nigh unapproachable, in its mingled dignity and
sweetness. It is impossible, it would be tedious, to
go into minute detail, or I could show you that
almost every line and every word, every turn of
thought and phrase, is governed by an exquisite grace
and tact beyond the reach of art. You will gain
some sense of the refined courtesy which breathes
through every sentence of this Letter, if you simply
reflect on the difficulties of the task to which the
Apostle addressed himself, and the completeness of
his victory over them. He was the common friend
of Philemon and Onesimus, each of whom thought
the other to have wronged him. He must conciliate
Philemon, yet commend Onesimus. He must
commend Onesimus, and yet not cloak his fault.
He has to affirm the brotherhood of slave and slaveowner, and to ask from a justly-offended master,
not only pardon, but fraternal kindness, for a fugitive and criminal slave. He might claim to speak
with authority, might be "bold to enjoin," since
Philemon owes him far more than Onesimus owes
Philemon; but he prefers to ask a favour, and "for
love's sake to beseech." He hardly likes to allude

to his own services; yet how, without some such allusion, which it is equally difficult to make and to avoid, can he get Philemon to feel that he asks less than he has given. He has to point out a duty, but would fain inspire a voluntary act of grace. It is because St. Paul has met these and kindred difficulties with the most sensitive and consummate tact; because by hints, by broken phrases, by half-suggestions, by touches of pathos, and even, as we shall see, by strokes of humour, he has succeeded in conveying all these contradictory moods of thought, without any sacrifice of truth or dignity, or the use of a single phrase at which the captious might take offence, that this letter has been singled out as the purest model of epistolary composition, and has been named by good judges " the Polite Epistle."

How generous, too, and how like the man, is the ardour with which he pleads the cause of the outcast! It is hardly possible to imagine any other Roman gentleman of that time so much as lifting one of his fingers to help a slave, much less a runaway slave who had embezzled his master's property. But how earnestly Paul pleads for him; how his

ardour mounts and grows! "I beseech thee for
my own child whom I have begotten in my bonds,
for Onesimus" (ver. 10). "Do thou receive him
that is *as my own heart*" (ver. 12), as "*a brother
beloved, very dear to me*" (ver. 16). "If thou art in
fellowship with me, welcome him *as myself*" (ver.
17). "If he hath wronged thee, or oweth thee
aught, *put that to my account.* I, Paul, write this
with my own hand"—so earnest am I, so bent on
winning grace for him—"*I will repay thee*" (vers.
18, 19). "Yea, brother, *let me have profit of thee :
refresh my heart* in Christ" (ver. 20). *I know
that thou wilt do even more than I say*" (ver. 21).
Is it not beautiful, is it not pathetic, to note the
intense beseeching earnestness which trembles in
these phrases, to mark the ingenious variations
through which love pursues its single prayer? He
pleads as for his own son, as for his dearest friend,
as for himself, as for his own heart. Could the force
of love go further? Is not this the Paul we know—
as fervid, as tender, as great of heart while he
pleads for this poor outcast as when he pleads for
Christ?

Nor, if we remember how even a slight stroke of humour deepens pathos, shall we feel either surprise or regret as we learn that St. Paul's humour* breaks through his most fervent appeals. Our English version gives no hint of the fact. Nor, indeed, is the humour at all profound. It is simply a pun, a play upon words; yet I can conceive that Paul uttered it with a somewhat sad and wistful face. The jest lies in the name of the slave. Onesimus means "profitable" or "useful:" because of the meaning of the word, it was a common name among the slaves of antiquity. In the tenth and eleventh verses of this Letter, Paul writes, "I beseech thee for my own child whom I have begotten in my bonds, for Onesimus"—or, as we should say, for *Profitable*,—"who was once *unprofitable* to thee, but now is *profitable* both to thee and to me." We can hardly pronounce the jest to

---

* A very striking essay might be written on the Humour of St. Paul. There are abundant materials for it. No one at all conversant with his Epistles in the Greek can doubt that a very strong vein of humour ran through his mind, or that he freely used this, as all other gifts, in the service of Christ. In the First Epistle to the Corinthians, for instance, he again and again takes up the admissions or boasts of the Corinthian converts, and holds them in the most ludicrous and absurd lights, that he may shame his readers out of their follies and sins.

be of singular excellence; but St. Paul finds it such an excellent good jest, that he recurs to it in the twentieth verse, " Yea, brother, let me have *profit* of thee." But whatever we may think of this play on words—and even the greatest wits sometimes stoop to these familiar touches—it is surely pleasant to conceive of the Apostle as thus unbending in his familiar intercourse with his friends, and as ingeniously blunting the edge of Philemon's resentment, by talking, as John Bunyan might have done, of " Master Profitable, who was once unprofitable, but who will henceforth deserve his name."

Hardly enough, perhaps, has been made of this point—that the humour of the Apostle covers his tact. He has to refer to the sin—the embezzlement—of Onesimus, that he may ask pardon for it. But how shall he refer to it so as at once to hurt the repentant slave as little as he may, and to placate his offended master? Philemon, as he recalled the offence of Onesimus, would be apt to frown. If the Apostle could so touch that offence as to make Philemon smile, much would be gained. Philemon could hardly but smile at the notion of

"Profitable" having been "unprofitable;" and thus the Apostle would have gained his end with him. He would also have gained his end with Onesimus: for how could his wound be more gently touched? how, if his offence must be recalled, could it be recalled more lightly and tenderly?

Nor must we omit to note the pure and high devotion which characterizes St. Paul's most familiar talk no less than his public utterances. Here, he is only writing, on a private affair, to a personal friend; he unbends into an innocent jest: but he opens his Letter with salutations and thanksgivings and prayers, and closes it with a benediction, as lofty and devout as though he were writing to a church on the profoundest mysteries of the Faith. The main body or substance of his Letter, moreover, is, as we shall presently see, most devout and religious. Under all its courtesies and jests and pathetic personal appeals, there lies this great argument—and it is *the* argument of the Letter—that there is a Christian "fellowship," or communion, of which Paul and Philemon and Onesimus are all

members; that if this fellowship is an effectual
energy, and not a mere name, they are all brethren;
that this new Christian relation overrides all other
relations; that in Christ Jesus there is neither Jew
nor Greek, neither Asiatic nor Roman, neither
master nor slave, bond nor free, but all are brethren
because *He* is Brother to all. It is this underlying
argument, which only crops up to the surface now
and then, that makes the Apostolic appeal so
cogent, so ardent, so pathetic, so effective.

And it is only this Christian fellowship, and our
deep sense of it, which will give the right tone to
all our speech, the right form to all our conduct.
We are apt to forget this, to think too little of the
shaping spirit of our life and too much of its outward forms. Take an illustration suggested by our
theme. As we read this Letter to Philemon, we
can hardly fail to ask ourselves, " How is it that
Christian men no longer correspond in this style?
When *we* write to a brother in the Faith, we send
him no Christian salutation or benediction, no
thanksgiving for the good already wrought in him

by the grace of God, no prayer that the fellowship
of our faith may grow more effectual and sweep a
wider range. We hardly ever do that : yet St. Paul
seems to have done it habitually, in his private notes
no less than in his public correspondence." True,
my brethren. Nevertheless, how foolish it would
be of us to copy his forms of correspondence instead
of seeking to share his spirit ! There are still
whole races of men—most of the Oriental races—
who use these devout forms as habitually as St. Paul
himself, and are in nothing the better for it, often
the worse. Let me read you a modern letter * of
this kind, omitting only a single sentence. It is
addressed by one Arab Prince to another, and runs
thus :—" In the Name of God, the Merciful, the
Compassionate, We, 'Obeyd-ebn-Rasheed, salute
you, O 'Abd-Allah, son of Feysulebn-Sa'ood :
Peace be upon you, and the mercy of God and His
blessings. . . . Now may God forbid that we
should hear of any evil having befallen you. We
salute also your Father Feysul, and your brothers,

* I take this "letter" from Palgrave's "Central Arabia," in which
charming book all the details to which I allude are given in full. See
vol. i. chap. v. p. 209.

and all your family, and anxiously await your news in answer. Peace be with you." That surely is a very pious and Apostolic letter. Yet it was written by a prince whose innumerable treacheries and murders had earned him the surname of "the Wolf:" and the omitted sentence charged two innocent travellers, an Englishman and a Syrian, with a crime punishable by death in the country for which they were just starting. With a courtly smile, and as a recommendation to favour, he gave them this pious treacherous letter, in which death and murder lurked under devout forms, and which would certainly have cost them their lives had they delivered it.

It would not be wise to lay too much stress, then, on the mere retention of pious forms and phrases, or to sigh for a return to Apostolic methods of correspondence. What we really want is *the Apostolic spirit*,—that courteous, generous, devout temper which gave beauty and completeness to all Paul did and said. Apart from that, in what stead will forms of devotion, however perfect, stand us ? Having that, we may, very safely, leave it to adopt or create its own forms. It is not the absence, whether from our letters or our lives, of gracious -standing forms corresponding to the salutations and benedictions, the prayers and thanksgivings of St. Paul's Epistles to his friends, which we need to deplore ; but the too frequent absence of that humble, devout, charitable spirit which should be ours if we are Christ's, and which, were it ours, would breathe through all our utterances and all our conduct. What we want is, not more leaves shaped after an antique ecclesiastical pattern, but more of that noble Christian life which brings forth ever new, and ever better, fruit.

II. "Christianity," said Mr. Canning, in one of the debates on the Emancipation of the West Indian Slaves, "grew up amidst the scenes of tyranny which are described in the sixth Satire of Juvenal. It recognized the institution of slavery. How can it be said to be essentially adverse to that institution ?" The question is of no slight moment, and should be fairly met. Nevertheless, it is not easy to meet it fairly. Not at all, however, because

D

we have any doubt that the Gospel of Christ is
" adverse " to " the institution of Slavery," but because we know it to be *essentially* adverse, adverse,
that is, *in essence* and substance rather than in outward form.   For on this, as on so many other points,
the Gospel furnishes us with no definite maxim, no
portable and unalterable rule of conduct; but it lays
down a general principle as large and flexible as
human life, and leaves us to apply that principle to
the varying conditions of humanity, to the changing
needs of the changing moment.   Now to master
and apply general principles requires an insight, a
patience, a loyalty to truth which few men attain,
or will be at the trouble to use.   Unskilled and
impatient, they, for the most part, crave definite
sharply-cut precepts which will apply themselves.
They must always have a pilot aboard who will
relieve them of the labour of thought, the burden of
responsibility.   Give them only the chart and compass of general principles, and they feel themselves
cast upon a troubled sea, whose paths are all unknown
to them, and whose waves cast up only mire and
dirt.   Nay more, they cannot see their brethren,

however patient and skilled, embark on this wide tossing sea, without instantly foreboding disaster and wreck. It is very much, I apprehend, because the Gospel lays down no sharp rigid rule on Slavery, and because men will not be at the pains to study those broad general principles which shade into all the conditions of human life, taking as well as giving colour, taking that they *may* give, that many excellent men have doubted whether the institution of Slavery is, or is not, essentially adverse to the Gospel of Christ. Let us understand, then, that if we would know " the mind of Christ" on this question, we are not to expect any definite authoritative maxim addressed to the social conditions of His time ; but a general principle, applicable to all times and conditions, which we shall not discover without some research, or master without some pains.

But though the Gospel only gives us a principle of this kind, we may see it at work, in the churches of Ephesus and Colossæ for instance, and rapidly producing a social revolution deeper and broader than was ever yet effected by mere rule or authority. Nay, in St. Paul's letter to Philemon, we have a

vivid and living picture illustrative of the action of
this principle, a picture in which we see it carried
to its last and fair result. It is in its handling of
Slavery indeed, that the interest of this Letter centres
and culminates. Here the general principle is not
only stated, but applied ; and in studying its application we shall gain our truest and deepest conception
of the principle itself.

What, then, was the condition of the slave in
classical times ? and how did the Gospel apply itself
to that condition ?

The slaves of classical antiquity were a class of
men degraded not only beyond any instance but
almost beyond the comprehension of modern times.
They were in the power of their masters even to
the severest form of death, nay, even to those un-
nameable insults sooner than submit to which any
man worthy of the name would be " blithe to find
the grave." They could own no property, nor hold
any sacred domestic relationship. Their time, their
faculties, their very persons, were not their own.
They had no standing in any legal court, and were
never examined except under torture. They were

beat and buffeted in wanton cruelty, or caressed to their dishonour: Epictetus, the Stoic philosopher,* for instance—who, like Onesimus, was a Phrygian slave, and like him, was now in the precincts of Nero's palace—had his leg broken by his master, who, for mere sport, began wrenching it this way and that. They were often compelled to fight with wild beasts in the arena, or were murdered by the gladiators to make a Roman holiday.† If they multiplied too rapidly, they were reduced by wholesale exter-

---

* Epictetus, born at Hierapolis in Phrygia, was, say *A. Gellius* and *Suidas,* slave to Epaphroditus, a freedman of the Emperor Nero, and the captain of his guard. Probably he was but a lad when Paul dwelt in his "hired house," awaiting Nero's caprice. Epictetus was the most Christian of the Stoic philosophers. Many of his sentences read as though they had been taken from our Lord's Sermon on the Mount, or from the Epistles of St. Paul. And I have sometimes thought that, while he was running about the Prætorium, he may have met his countryman, Onesimus, have been drawn by him into the hut of the Apostle, and heard so much of the truth as it is in Jesus as gave a tone to his subsequent meditations.

The anecdote referred to in the text we owe to Origen (Orig. cont. Cels. lib. vii.). As he tells it, it is an almost incredible instance of patient stoicism. According to the admiring Father, Epaphroditus one day took to violently wrenching his slave's leg about in frolic. Epictetus, without any appearance of passion, said to him with a smile, "If you go on, sir, you will break my leg." What he foresaw came to pass. And then, in the same quiet tone, he added, "Did I not tell you, sir, that you would break my leg?" The philosophic slave halted to his tomb. Long before his death, however, he became a freedman, and taught his pure lofty tenets to a large and noble audience.

† "Whenever the Roman entered his dwelling, the slave chained in the doorway, the thongs hanging from the stairs, the marks of the iron and the cord on the face of his domestics, all impressed him with the feeling

minations, and even in the noblest and most heroic states of Greece, it was reckoned an evening's pastime for the free youth to thin their numbers by an indiscriminate and bloody onslaught. Cato the Censor, held to be the most just and honourable of the Romans, habitually turned out slaves, who had grown old and feeble in his service, to die in the street, or suffered them to starve outright beneath his roof. And in this most miserable class there were many who were not " to the manner born; " men of noble lineage and learned culture, women reared in the tender seclusion of refined luxurious homes: and these, of all " the most deject and wretched " taken captive in war, lay at the mercy of men who knew no mercy for slaves, and were compelled to minister to their brutal lusts, or were tortured to death to glut their caprice.

that he was a despot himself; for despot and master were only other words for the same fearful thing, the irresponsible owner of a horde of human chattels. When he seated himself in the circus, and beheld the combats of men with beasts, or of men with their fellow-men, when he smelt the reeking fumes of blood which saffron odours could not allay, heard the groans of the wounded, and, appealed to with the last look of despair, gave recklessly the sign for slaughter, he could not but be conscious of the same glow of pleasurable excitement at the sight of death and torture which is ascribed to the most ferocious of tyrants.—Merivale's " History of the Roman Empire," vol. vi. chap. liv. p. 399.

With these unhappy creatures St. Paul, as he travelled from city to city, was constantly brought into contact. And to a man of so humane and generous a temper, his quick sensibility and burning indignation against injustice coming to the aid of the general Hebrew resentment against slavery,* their miserable estate must have caused many pangs. Nor was it only his personal and national sensibilities that were touched and offended, but also his zeal for Christ,

---

* It was a frequent habit among the Jews, as we learn from many passages in the Old Testament, to purchase slaves or servants. But we are not to suppose that the Hebrew servitude bore any resemblance to the slavery of Greece and Rome. Ginsburg, himself a Jew, and therefore speaking with some natural indignation, has a capital note on this point, in his "Coheleth," pp. 282—4. I subjoin an abstract of his argument. The Hebrews had no name for a slave, which implied that he was a mere *thing*, or chattel. עֶבֶד, the common Hebrew name for a slave or servant, means a *labourer*, and is often applied to the greatest prophets and kings : while the Greek δοῦλος, means *one who is bound or chained*, and the Latin *mancipium* means *captured goods* (I think Mr. Ginsburg will find that the root idea of *mancipium* is *that which is bought, property*, not *plunder* : this, however, does not affect his argument). These names fairly denote the characteristic differences between Hebrew and classical slavery. The Hebrew servant was acknowledged to be a man, in the image of God. He worked with his master, and with him kept the Sabbath and sacred festivals, which released him from labour nearly half his time. The law provided that he should be instructed in morals and religion. If he escaped from his master, he could not be delivered up to him by the inhabitants of the city in which he took refuge. His personal rights were protected by the law : if he lost the use of any limb or organ of the body, through the brutality of his master, he was immediately manumitted ; if he was killed, his master was tried for murder. He might marry his master's daughter : *his* daughter often married his master's son. If he were an Israelite, he was still regarded as a citizen, and a *hireling*,—could acquire property, therefore, and purchase his freedom. If he did not purchase it, it was given him in

and for the welfare and honour of the Church. He
had so learned Christ as to hold every man his
brother, as that nothing human was alien to him.
He believed that there lay before every soul of man
possibilities of recovery, of redemption, of holiness;
that the most abject might become noble; the most
sinful, pure. How, then, could he endure to see
any whose nature Christ had shared, and for whose
redemption Christ had died, condemned to a condi-

the seventh year; and when he was enfranchised his master was enjoined
to "furnish him liberally out of the flock, and the barn, and the winepress,"
that he might make a hopeful start in life.

Contrast with this humane conception and treatment of the Hebrew
slave, the conception and treatment of the classical slave. Aristotle defines
him as "a living and working tool;" Plato describes him as a being who
had "nothing healthy in his soul," as of "a race in which men possessing
any intellect ought never to trust," as "not to be spoken to as a free
man." Homer sings—

"Half their mind wide-seeing Jove has ta'en
From men, whose doom has Slavery's day brought on."

If the classical slave escaped, no refuge was open to him, the master pursued him wherever he pleased, and when he caught him, branded him,
often on the face, with a hot iron. He had no personal or legal rights;
his very life stood in the hazard of his master's whim. He was a mere
chattel, not a man, and might be flung aside the very moment he ceased
to be of use. Ginsburg gives his authorities for each of these statements,
and has, I think, conclusively proved that the classical slavery could only
inspire loathing and resentment in the Hebrew mind. Merivale, the his-
torian, is of the same mind with the learned commentator. "The social
relations (of the Jews) seem to have been unusually pure, those above all
of master and servant were natural and kindly. Slavery among the Jews
was so confined in its extent and so mild in practice, so guarded by law and
custom, as to become a real source of strength instead of weakness to the
commonwealth."—"Hist. Rom. Emp.," vol. vii. chap. lix. p. 190.

tion more foul, and wretched, and hopeless than that of the brutes? Above all, how could he bear to see those who were of like faith with him, who held, as he held, every man to be brother to Jesus and a son of God, guilty of this monstrous wrong, and retaining brethren in the abject conditions of slavery, in which virtue was well-nigh impossible? For *them* to do that, was to deny the fundamental truths of the Christian faith : it was to resist the impulses of that charity which is of all Christian graces the top and crown.

These feelings and convictions seem to have grown in force during the two years St. Paul dwelt at Rome. In the letters he wrote at this period—the Epistles to the Ephesians and the Colossians, as well as that to Philemon—he gives special prominence to the question of Slavery ;* and by his injunctions to both slaves and masters endeavours, at least, to alleviate the rigours of bondage. There was more than one reason why this subject should be much in his thoughts. One reason was this : We

---

* Ephesians vi. 5—9. Colossians iii. 22 to iv. 1. Both these Epistles were written during St. Paul's imprisonment at Rome.

learn from Tacitus,* that, in the very year of St. Paul's arrival in Rome, there occurred a frightful illustration of the infamous and cruel injustice with which slaves were treated in the metropolis of the world. Pedanius Secundus, prefect of the city, was killed by one of his slaves; and, in accordance with the wicked law of the time, the whole body of them, amounting to a vast multitude of men, women, and children, were publicly tortured to death, although innocent, and acknowledged to be innocent, of any complicity in the crime for which they suffered. An atrocity such as this could not fail to make a profound impression on the mind of the Apostle, an impression as painful as it was profound. And when, soon afterward, Onesimus told him *his* tale, that impression would be deepened; it would grow more painful and absorbing. Onesimus devoted himself to the service of the fettered Apostle, and displayed natural capacities and graces of character which won his heart. He loved him as his own son. Yet this man, so capable, so grateful, so

* Ann. xiv. 42—45.

eager to serve, was a slave; and had been so degraded by his abject condition that, in a moment of
temptation, he had embezzled his master's goods,
although, doubtless, that master, a Christian of fine
character and high standing, had been as considerate
and kind as a slaveowner could be.

With his keen far-reaching intellect, St. Paul
could not but see that there was something fatally
wrong in this social relation ; that, whatever leni-
tives and palliatives might be applied to it, it could
only, being itself an evil, bring forth evil fruit. Yet
how apply the only sovereign and complete remedy?
Slavery was an established institution of the time ;
it was interwoven with all the relations and interests
—domestic, civic, political—of society. To pluck
it suddenly out would be to imperil the whole fabric
—probably, to destroy it. To command every
master to manumit his slaves, and urge every slave
to strike a blow for freedom, would virtually be to
proclaim a servile war, which would breed new
horrors, and which must end either in embittering
the bitter condition of the slaves, or, should they
achieve an almost impossible victory, in the exter-

mination or bondage of their masters. Now St.
Paul was of a statesmanlike sagacity as well as of
an Apostolic fervour : and therefore he hated the
wasteful " falsehood of extremes." In his public
Epistles he endeavoured to mitigate the evil which
as yet—and because it entangled in its embraces
much that was good—it would not be safe to
destroy. He urged masters to remember that _they_
had " a Master in heaven," to treat their slaves
"with justice and equity," to " spare threats," and
to do them good. And he urged slaves to remember that they might " serve the Lord Christ " in
serving their masters, and that if they did all things
" as unto the Lord," they would rob even their
servile condition of its deadly sting. In short, he
taught the common _manhood_ of slaves and masters,
their common _brotherhood_ in Him " in whom is
neither bond nor free ;" and thus raised the Christian bondman from the deep degradation of the
classical slavery to at least the level of the Hebrew
servitude.

To young and ardent minds this may seem, as
indeed it often has seemed, a timid and unworthy

policy : for they cannot endure that the evils they denounce should be tolerated, even for an instant.* Their motto is, " Let justice be done though the heavens should fall !" I can only remind them that were strict immediate justice done, the heavens *would* fall, and crush the earth which now they bless. Happily for them and for us, He who sitteth on the circle of the heavens hath long patience. He is very pitiful, and of a most tender mercy, or our shrift would be short, our doom intolerable. And therefore, whatever we may think of it, it is often our duty and wisdom to let the evil and the good seed grow together, since we often cannot pluck up the one without uprooting the other ; and to leave the separation of the tares from the wheat in the hands

---

* Schiller, in a well-known passage, sets forth the contrast between the rash revolutionary humour of ardent all-assailing youth and the gradual tentative method of ripe experience and practised wisdom, under very happy figures :—

> The way of Order, though it lead through windings,
> Is the best.   Right forward goes the lightning,
> And the cannon-ball ; quick, by the nearest path,
> They come, op'ning with murderous crash their way,
> To blast and ruin !   My son, the quiet road
> Which men frequent, where peace and blessings travel,
> Follows the river's course, the valley's bendings ;
> Modest skirts the corn-field and the vineyard,
> Revering property's appointed bounds ;
> And leading safe, though slower, to the mark.

Wallenstein, Art I., Scene 4.

of the Great Husbandman. This was the course
St. Paul took, the duty he recognized. Hating the
evil as hotly as we can hate it, he saw that he could
not suddenly and forcibly root it out without doing
even a greater mischief than that he was fain to
destroy; and, therefore, he bade men keep under
the evil growths as strictly as they could, since at
present it would not be safe to extirpate them.

But, not content with this, he also set himself to
plant and foster good growths, which might be very
safely left to check their evil rivals. In his Epistles
to the Ephesians and Colossians he affirmed the
common manhood, and the common brotherhood,
of slaves and masters in Christ Jesus; and these
were principles which, as they grew and expanded,
were sure to overtop and stifle the evil he deplored.
And, in his Letter to Philemon, he repeats his argument in a new form and raised to a higher power.
As he revolved the case of Onesimus, seeking how
he might best assail an institution which already
threatened both the purity and the peace of the
Church, groping on all sides if haply he might find
some axe to lay to the very root of the evil, he lit

upon a weapon of heavenly temper and force.
This was what was then called " the fellowship,"
a word whose meaning we have naturally forgotten,
since we have lost so much of the spirit; but
which, so soon as we understand it, we shall find
to be simply the principles of a common humanity
and a Christian brotherhood raised to their highest
expression, and invested with an added sanctity.

In the primitive time, then, in the days that
followed the first Christian Pentecost, that which
seems to have struck the new converts as no less
novel and original than " the teaching of the
Apostles," was the sort of life which obtained
among them and their adherents.* While the Lord
Jesus was still with them, the Apostles had formed
a moving household, going with Him whithersoever
He went, dwelling where He dwelt, eating of one
table with Him. So, too, the disciples outside the
Apostolic circle appear to have regarded themselves
as members of His family, and to have met His

---

* " They," *i. e.*, the Pentecostal converts, " stedfastly addicted themselves
to the teaching of the Apostles, *and to the fellowship*, and to the breaking
of the bread, and t the times of prayer."—Acts ii. 42.

immediate followers as brothers and sisters, not simply as fellow-citizens or fellow-worshippers. And when He went up on high, the little company of believers in Jerusalem "continued with one accord in one place," living together on pleasant equal terms as members of one family—a family whose ties were drawn very close by the bitter and general enmity to which they were exposed from without. This happy "fellowship" of kindred hearts was the spectacle which took, and held, the eyes of the three thousand converts. *They* were strangers out of every nation under heaven, separated from each other by diversities of race and habit and tongue. Though they were of one faith, —for they were all either Jews or proselytes—their faith was but a slack bond of union. The temple was a scene of strife between warring sects and factions. Galilean and Judean, Hellenist and Hebrew, Pharisee and Sadducee, Herodian, Sanhedrist, and Roman partisan wrangled among themselves and with each other. Every clique, every school, every faction, every race had its separate synagogue where they worshipped apart.

Is it any wonder that men whose very religion was
a dispute, and whose most solemn acts of worship
often broke into bloody frays, when they saw the
little band of Christians, " of one heart and mind,"
meeting " with one accord in one place," were
arrested by a spectacle so singular, attracted by a
"fellowship" so pure and tender and harmonious?
Here were " a hundred and twenty" men and
women of different races, grades, cultures, living
together not only in an unbroken concord of worship and affection, but in a holy enthusiasm of love
which made each the servant of all, and forbad any
one of them to say that aught of the things which
he possessed was his own! With what an eager
gladness would the strangers out of every nation
addict themselves to such a fellowship as this, and
find themselves welcomed into a family and possessed of a home quick with love and goodwill!

This, then, was " the fellowship," the warm,
sacred " communion" of the primitive Church,
which, with the cords of its strong tender humanity,
drew the new converts to its bosom and inspired
them with a spirit akin to its own.

E

What was the secret of it? It was the vivid
absorbing consciousness of a common life in Christ.
He had come to teach a new faith, and give a new
commandment,—the faith, a holy trust in the redeeming love of God, the Father of all men,—the
commandment, an injunction to love one another
on the ground of a common humanity, a common
redemption, a common brotherhood. He had
illustrated this faith by becoming the sacrifice of
our redemption. He had kept this commandment
by loving all men with a love which the many
waters of a Divine grief could not quench. His Spirit,
the Spirit of love and self-sacrifice, had descended
on those who followed Him, and " filled " them
with the grace which dwelt in Him. Like Him,
they trusted in God the universal Father : like Him,
they loved every man his brother. How could
they but love and serve each other when one life
beat in every breast, and in serving each other they
served Him from whom their life sprang ? Compared
with this sacred unity, what was the national bond,
or even the family tie ? If to have derived flesh
and blood from a common family source, or to have

common national interests, and habits, and aims, were much; how much more was it to have derived the life of the spirit from the Christ in whom their brethren lived, and to have all their eternal habits, and interests, and aims in common!

To this " fellowship," which, after all, and, as we have just seen, is but the highest and most sacred expression of our common humanity and common brotherhood, the Apostles perpetually appeal, when they would urge their disciples to advanced stages of thought and action. It takes many forms. It is " the fellowship of the body—of the blood—of the life—of the sufferings of Christ:" it is " the fellowship of the light—of the faith—of the Spirit—of the saints." But, always and everywhere, it implies the happy equal intercourse of redeemed men who have been gathered into one family, one household,—a household and family in which the least are greatest, and the strongest serve, and the most eminent are the most lowly.

Now it is to this " fellowship " that St. Paul appeals in his Letter to Philemon. The appeal lies

at the basis of his whole argument, but more than
once it comes to the surface and finds clear expression.   Thus, in ver. 6, he prays that " *the fellowship* of " Philemon's " faith *may become effectual in
the full knowledge of every good thing which is in us,*"
to the glory of Christ Jesus.   And the meaning of
the prayer is, that the community of thought and
feeling which already exists between them—*i. e.,*
between Paul and Philemon — may first become
" an energy," and find its appropriate expression in
all good works, not remain a mere concord of
thought and sentiment, but pass on into a holy
activity ; and then, that this active community of
Christian sentiment and opinion may become perfect and complete, Philemon, advancing to the
furthest limit Paul has reached—to " the full
knowledge of every good thing which is in " the
Apostle, that so, keeping step and pace the one with
the other, they may both mind the same things and
be moved by the same affections toward the same
persons.   This is the general meaning of the
prayer ; but of course the Apostle had a particular
application of it in his thoughts.   Paul had learned

to love Onesimus, whom, as yet, Philemon held in distrust and disfavour. Paul regarded him, not only as a slave, but as a brother beloved, very dear to him (ver. 16); while to Philemon he was not a brother, but only a slave. And what the Apostle really intends in his prayer is, that Philemon should learn to share his feeling for Onesimus. He is quite sure that his love for the repentant slave is a " good thing:" and, as Philemon shares so many other good things with him, he would have him share this also. Their " fellowship " covers much ; let it cover all. He longs to feel that their sympathy and communion are complete. The desire grows upon him as he writes. And in the 17th verse, he adds : " *If thou art in fellowship with me, welcome him (Onesimus) as myself* "— implying that their fellowship could hardly be genuine and sincere unless, at least on this matter, Philemon should think and sympathize with him. To St. Paul it appears that it will be nothing short of a breach in their communion if, while he regards Onesimus as a dear brother, Philemon regards him as a runaway and felonious slave.

Our poet Tennyson sings :—

> In Love, if Love be Love, if Love be ours,
> Faith and unfaith can ne'er be *equal* powers :
> Unfaith in aught is want of faith in all.

> It is the little rift within the lute,
> That by and by will make the music mute,
> And, ever widening, slowly silence all.

And I do not know that we can have a better illustration of the Apostle's feeling. To his fervent and excited heart it seems as though, if Philemon's fellowship with him is not complete, answering point to point through its whole compass and range, it is no true fellowship at all. He virtually says : " We agree in much. There are whole broad tracts of thought thrown open to us by the Gospel of Christ in which we are of one mind. We love God, and Christ, and the Church ; we make many sacrifices that we may serve them : but, though we have all this in common, could I suppose that we should differ in thought and affection about this poor slave, that you should fail to recognize a brother in him who is as my own child to me; *that*, though to many it might seem a very small thing, would be so fatal a breach in our communion as would well-nigh break my heart : it would be a discordant note which would swell till it overpowered all the harmony of our love : it would be ' the rift within the lute '—little at first, perhaps, but slowly widening till all its music were hushed."

In St. Paul's judgment, then—and in this matter he is a higher authority than even Mr. Canning—the institution of slavery was " essentially adverse " to the Gospel of Christ, since it was a fatal breach in the Christian fellowship. In his public Epistles, he might be content, and that for very good reasons, to give only counsels of prudence and mutual goodwill. He might advise slaves to patience, obedience, and that divine eye-service which would redeem them from the fear of man : he might advise masters to consideration, forbearance, gentleness, and a dutiful remembrance of *their* Master in heaven.* But in a private letter to Philemon and Onesimus, his personal friends, he

* I have sometimes thought that St. Paul may have habitually called himself " *a slave* of the Lord Jesus Christ," both to remind the slaves in the Church that their servile condition need not impair their true dignity and freedom, and to remind masters of the considerate kindness which even a slave might claim at their hands.

could more fully open his mind. And to these he says, in effect :—" The real question is, Are you brothers in Christ ? Is this Christian brotherhood to be a real ' energy,' an effective power, or is it not ? Are we to talk of ' *the fellowship*,' yet not to acknowledge each other as *fellows*, as equals, before our common Lord ? Is the communion of the faith to cover only acts of public worship, or is it to extend to all the relations, and intercourses, and duties of life ? What is this ' fellowship ' worth, if you, Philemon, may regard as lawful what I condemn as a sin against brotherhood ; if you may whip, and brand, and torture him who is ' as my own heart ' ? What is this ' fellowship' worth, if you, Philemon, may sit at one board with Onesimus, eat of one loaf, drink of one cup, sing one psalm, and say ' Amen ' to his prayer ; and then rise from your common worship to make his life bitter to him with toil and cruel bondage ? When I come to you, and I hope shortly to be given to your prayers, am I to find one brother using his freedom to put the other brother in chains ? Must I and Archippus, your son, who by then will have

further instructed Onesimus in the heavenly hopes
of the Gospel, rise from your hospitable table to
comfort the poor slave who trembles under your
displeasure? or are we all, you and I, Archippus
and Onesimus, to be true brothers in Christ, com-
forting and serving each other in the Lord?"

Now it is very easy to say that St. Paul did not
condemn slavery, and thus connived at vice when it
was strong and popular: but *can* we say it when
once we have followed out the argument of this
Letter? He dared not, though he dare do whatever
might become a man and an apostle, demand the
instant enfranchisement of all who were held in
slavery, lest a worse thing should come in its place.
But though he did not press for its immediate abolition, or urge on a servile war, does he not teach a
truth which ultimately, as soon indeed as it was understood, cut up slavery by the very roots?* Is it

* No candid reader of ecclesiastical history will either deny that even
from the first the Gospel greatly ameliorated the condition of the slaves of
Christian masters, or claim that its tru · bearing on this question was recognized by the Church for many centuries. Long after St. Paul had entered
on his rest, Christians, and even the clergy, held their brethren and sisters
in bondage. Yet manumission grew more common as the years passed;

not this doctrine of "the Christian fellowship," as expounded and enforced by him, which has, in these last days, proved itself the conqueror of slavery, and in all ages has been the strength of those who have stood up for the weak against the strong and for the poor against the oppressions of wealth ?

It is because the Roman Church, with all its heresies, has held fast to " the fellowship," refusing to recognize distinctions of race and class in the Church, and holding all her capable sons eligible to any—even the highest—office or dignity : it is, at least in part, because of this, that she has survived so many assaults, and still wields so great a power in the earth.   It is because, much as we pride our-selves on holding the primitive doctrine and main-taining the primitive order, *we* have so largely let this " fellowship " slip from our hands, that we are

and it is significant that in one of, the earliest rescripts of Constantine, the first Christian emperor,—that which set apart the first day of the week for worship—it was provided that the only purpose for which the legal courts might be opened on Sunday was the manumission of slaves (Cod. Theodos. II. viii. 1).   Subsequent edicts made it penal to steal infants for slaves—a common practice,—or to punish slaves to excess, or to torture them to death ; though the rudeness of the times still permitted much that the Gospel condemns.

so weak and do so little to win men to our communion. *Communion!* Why, what communion is
there among us? Can we affirm that the sense of
Christian brotherhood is as strong in us as even the
ties of neighbourhood, or political party, or natural
kinship? How many of us feel an inward fire of
love for all who are one with us in Christ? How
many of us would do as much to serve even a member of the same church as we would to serve a
neighbour with whom we were intimate, or to
secure the election of a member of Parliament who
held our political views? Look around you.
" Mark them which cause divisions." How many
they are! On what slight grounds, on what slight
pretexts even, will they disturb the peace of the
Church! With what arrogance they judge and
condemn brethren who are at least as wise as they
are, and whose lives are at least as pure as theirs!
How much do they care for " the fellowship " when
once it is put in competition with their whims, their
prejudices, their preferences?

And yet they and we are loud in our complaints
that men are not won to the faith of Christ; that

even of those who are won many decline to join the Christian fellowship ! Had we not better leave off prating about " the fellowship " till we have something a little more like " fellowship " to show ? When, like the early converts, we are with one accord in one place : when those who are without, as they peer wistfully through door and casement, see a Christian family, whose members are all aglow with love and goodwill, dwelling together in the happiness of mutual service and self-sacrifice : when we can make them feel that they will find *a home* with us, a true home, a home more free and pure and tender than they can find elsewhere : when the kindly household warmth shines through all windows, and streams guiding and inviting rays into the darkness without : then, if the Divine promises be true, and the Divine laws hold their course, there will be a crowd of eager applicants for admission ; our Father's house will be filled, and His bountiful table furnished with guests.

To hasten which happy consummation, let us each do what, and all, he can.

THE EPISTLE TO PHILEMON

by

A. H. Drysdale

Foreword by
Dr. Cyril J. Barber

Klock & Klock Christian Publishers, Inc.
2527 Girard Avenue North
Minneapolis, Minnesota 55411

This edition copied from
The Religious Tract Society
London, 1925
Third Edition

ISBN: 0-86524-134-1

Printed by Klock & Klock in the U.S.A.
1982 Reprint

CONTENTS

INTRODUCTION

TRANSLATION AND PARAPHRASE

EXPOSITION

ADDRESS AND SALUTATION

5

Contents

Contents

INTRODUCTION

I

SPECIAL CHARACTER OF THE EPISTLE

A TOUCHING story underlies this Epistle to Philemon. St Paul's
A subtle argument on behalf of a bondman runs shortest
through it, along with a series of the most melting Letter.
appeals. Add to this the wealth of noble sentiment
which Paul's rich nature is inspired to pour into it,
and the result lies before us in as exquisite a letter
as was ever penned in so few words.

Of its twenty-five short verses we may fitly say:

'They live, they speak, they breathe what *love* inspires,
Warm from the soul and faithful to its fires.'

The Epistle is very brief—the briefest, indeed, of
Paul's letters—but it is instinct with a peculiar
energy and pathos that amply entitle it to share in
the verdict which was extorted from his unfriendly
critics at Corinth : 'His letters, say they, are weighty
and powerful' (2 Cor. x. 10).

From a merely literary or æsthetic point of view the Its matchless
present one has commanded for itself an admiration Grace.
all its own. This is due not so much to any finish
in its style—it is too condensed and earnest to be
artificially precise—but to the delicate tact of its
address, the consummate grace of its rhetoric, and

The Epistle of St Paul to Philemon

especially the matchless refinement of Christian thought and feeling that breathes through every line.

Bishop Smalridge, Serm. 39.

There is but one opinion of its unique merits. They are thus summed up by an old writer, well qualified to judge: 'I dare be bold to say there is not extant in all the monuments of ancient and modern oratory a more perfect pattern of persuasive eloquence than is this short Epistle of St Paul.' It would be easy to present a long array of similar eulogiums. Writers of all ages have seemed to vie with each other in paying this Epistle the most golden tributes: 'Cicero never wrote with greater eloquence,' says Erasmus, characteristically. 'A masterpiece of its kind' (Doddridge). 'More cogently and courteously no man could plead' (Eichhorn). 'A small yet true *chef-d'œuvre* of the art of letter-writing' (Renan).

Such testimonies might be indefinitely multiplied from the most opposite quarters—even from the most vehement impugners of supernatural inspiration.

Demonstrably authentic and genuine.

That it is really a production of the apostle whose name it bears admits of no manner of doubt. So strong are both the external and internal evidences, that there is a unanimity on the point well-nigh perfect. Amid even the fearless rationalistic criticism of the day (whose operation has not been without its value, although its motto has too much resembled the old savage war-cry,

'Take thought, and spare nought;'

and though like Nature, as the poet paints it, 'red in tooth and claw,' it has shown ruthless delight in

12

Special Character of the Epistle

tearing to pieces many a venerable tradition), this Epistle to Philemon has stood the most rigorous cross-examination, and come out of the ordeal with its authenticity and genuineness indisputably established.

Indeed, the external or historical evidence for Paul's authorship is far too weighty to have been ever impugned. Only twice has even the feeblest measure of doubt been expressed on internal grounds. A few in the fourth century appear to have thought the letter was not sufficiently edifying, and possibly, therefore, not Paul's, while it has been reserved for one of the chief modern sceptical critics to suggest that as the style and story are almost too fine to be real, the letter is perhaps a well-designed effort of fancy to inculcate some noble Christian lessons, and therefore not likely to be St Paul's, if founded or fiction!

'The Epistle too unedifying to be worthy of Paul,' suggests the one. 'Too exquisite and engaging to be anything else than the outcome of a gospel romance,' whispers the other. Such opposite perversities may well be left to do the work of self-refutation. Renan's conclusion may be accepted as the universal one, and his decisiveness of tone speaks volumes; 'Peu de pages ont un accent de sincerité aussi prononcé. *Paul seul*, autant qu'il semble, a pu écrire ce petit chef-d'œuvre.' 'So far as appears, *Paul alone* can have written this little masterpiece.'

No one will suppose—in fact, no one has ever been foolish enough to suppose — that Timothy was in any sense joint author, because he is so closely

Marginal notes:

Paul's sole authorship established.

See the 'Introduction critique des documents originaux,' prefixed to his *St Paul*.

The Epistle of St Paul to Philemon

associated with the apostle: 'Paul, a prisoner of Jesus Christ, and Timothy the brother.' For the use of the *singular* first personal pronoun throughout makes Paul's exclusive authorship sufficiently clear. Indeed, it is a remarkable circumstance that there is *no plural verb* in the whole Epistle, according to the best Greek text.

A private or unofficial Letter. Among the writings of the apostle this occupies a place quite by itself. It is a letter of personal friendship, the only specimen we have of what may be regarded as Paul's strictly private correspondence. All his other Epistles are official, endorsed as it were with the sign-manual and seal of apostolic authoritativeness, whether addressed to Churches or, like the Pastoral Epistles, to individuals in their public capacity.

Here, however, we have a truly private letter, addressed in an avowedly unofficial tone to a personal acquaintance, about a purely domestic occurrence, and despatched with the same messenger that bore a public letter to the general Church where the apostle's friend was a worthy member.

On domestic and social affairs. This precious relic has been preserved from the mass of similar letters written by Paul to other friends in various parts of the world, probably for much the same reasons which have led to a selection of his great sermons, like that on Mars' Hill, or the Address to the Elders of Ephesus, being chosen to fill the place they do in Holy Writ, while the rest were suffered to pass into oblivion. As suitable specimens of inspired eloquence they have embalmed for us, as in the purest amber, not a few of the

14

Special Character of the Epistle

most exquisite filaments of sacred truth that have
no counterpart to themselves in Scripture. So has
this Epistle been set among the archives and
standards of apostolic literature on account of its
intrinsic fitness to fill up a hiatus in apostolic
correspondence as an inspired guide to individuals
and households in the application of Christian
principles to ordinary domestic and social affairs.

There is not much room for diversity of opinion
on the *date* and *birth-place* of the letter. It is
universally regarded as belonging to the apostle's
first captivity.

This lasted, however, upwards of four years— Time and
two of them in Cæsarea and two in Rome. Which place of
of these places should be fixed on? A few have writing.
felt disposed, we cannot but think for very insufficient
reasons, to say Cæsarea; but the great bulk of
authorities agree, on fairly conclusive evidence, that
as Paul anticipates with certainty a speedy release
(ver. 22), he wrote it from Rome a little before he
was set at liberty (A.D. 63 or early in 64), when
also we must date his Epistles to the Colossians,
Ephesians, and Philippians.

In what precise order these four followed each
other cannot be determined, though a plausible
claim might be set up for Philemon being the *first*
of the group. An interest attaches to it, as at all
events an early specimen—if not the earliest—in
that goodly array of what may be called the prison-
literature of the Church—a literature not less rich
in its legacies than unpropitious in its opportunities.
Apart from Scripture itself, and besides such out-

15

The Epistle of St Paul to Philemon

standing glories of this order as Luther's *New Testament Translation,* from the friendly confinement of the Wartburg, or the immortal dreamer's *Pilgrim's Progress,* we may not unfitly recall a few *minor* relics of devout prisoners, like the noble letters of Chrysostom in exile at Cucucus, which Gibbon contrasts so favourably with the querulous Epistles of Cicero under similar circumstances ; or Savonarola's *Christian Life and Commentaries* on certain Psalms from his Florentine cell : or the beautiful Latin metrical version of the Psalms, by George Buchanan, many of them composed in the Portuguese Inquisition ; or John's Frith's *Lyttle Treatise* on the Lord's Supper from the Tower of London 1533 ; or the *Truth of Christianity,* by Hugo Grotius, in the Castle of Loevestein (Louvain); or the *Letters* of Samuel Rutherford, from what he quaintly and cheerily calls 'Christ's *Palace* in Aberdeen ;' or William Penn's *No Cross, no Crown,* from the Tower in 1669 ; or the *Hymns* of Madame Guyon, 1689, familiar, some of them, through Cowper's translations, from her prison of Vincennes. 'As if I were a bird,' she says, 'whom the Lord has placed in a cage with nothing to do but sing.' These are but random recollections of multitudes of kindred memorials by kindred sufferers, 'of whom the world was not worthy.'

In singular contrast to all ordinary prison associations, we have to think of this Epistle as a model— an enduring model of the most refined courtesy. For it has long been known by the name of *The Polite Epistle*—a politeness very different from mere

16

Special Character of the Epistle

conventional civility, as far removed by its tone of cordial sincerity from mere hollow etiquette as by its tenderness of expression from the hardness of blunted feeling.

But it is more, much more, than a specimen of high-bred culture and delicacy of sentiment. It is a happy record of some of the finest features of Paul's Christian nature.

Had it only illustrated his powers of winning Why so address and his command of an all but irresistible carefully preserved. power of persuasiveness, it had probably not been preserved in its present place. But what a precious heritage it becomes for all time as a felicitous photograph of the finer features of his disposition ; a remarkable transcript of the Christian spirit at its very best; an exquisitely chased casket enclosing the richly jewelled coronet of heavenly culture to which Paul's nature had attained under the manifold workings of Divine grace! The ideal of a Christian gentleman finds here a noble realisation. Two corroborative passages, out of many similar ones, may be interesting for their writers' sakes, and for being so very characteristic of two such different types of men.

'The politeness of modern society is in many Dr respects the embodiment of the Christian graces. It Chalmers, *Sabbath* may be, and I fear generally is, the body without the *Bible* spirit: but that it should express what it does is *Readings.* itself an homage, the homage at least of its forms, to the substantial virtues of the gospel of Jesus Christ. When I contrast such a chivalrous disposition of so much generosity, and so much gentleness as is here made, with the rudeness of that age, I cannot but

B 17

The Epistle of St Paul to Philemon

look on the outpeering quality of this Epistle, before that of all other specimens that have come down to us, as another and most interesting contribution to the evidence daily accumulating on our view, in behalf of the Divine origin of our faith.'

Dr John Henry Newman. 'There is not any one of those refinements and delicacies of feeling which are the result of advanced civilisation, not any one of those proprieties and embellishments of conduct in which the cultivated intellect delights, but Paul is a pattern of it, in the midst of that assemblage of other supernatural excellences which is the common endowment of apostles and saints.'

Superb ideal of Christian Character. How that ideal is produced—how Christianity makes the 'highest style of man' — is amply illustrated throughout the Epistle, abounding as it does in all the vital elements of gospel faith and practice.

We shall not, of course, find in this private letter the array of doctrinal statements, so fully developed in the public epistles. But we are not permitted to mourn their absence, for, far from being absent, they are even more conspicuous than verbal expression almost could make them, transfigured into a living radiance from which gleams forth 'a glory that excelleth.'

Warmly Evangelical in tone. We may learn the tone of the Epistle from such facts as these—there are no fewer than *eleven* references to the Lord Jesus by name, while the specially significant phrase '*in Christ Jesus*' occurs oftener than in the same number of verses anywhere else in Scripture.

18

Special Character of the Epistle

Christ is prominently held up as the grand object of gospel faith and the only source of spiritual life; while this faith, if real, must invariably work by love, and attest its presence by practical Christian fellowship, forgivingness, and beneficence.

The Epistle is full of such evangelical principles as are suggested by the name of God as 'Father,' Christ Jesus as 'Lord,' each Christian 'a saint,' and every saint 'a brother beloved,' and by the frequent recurrence of *key-words*, like 'grace and peace,' 'prayer,' 'faith,' 'love,' and 'joy.' *Its key-words, spirit and life.*

The worth of the letter consists not so much in what it inculcates as what it *exemplifies*.

It is in this way, as from the hem of Christ's garment, a 'virtue goes out of it.' Its whole contents realise in a pre-eminent degree those influences which the Lord attaches to His own personal sayings: 'The words that I speak unto you, they are spirit and they are life.' For here we find the most subtle products of that 'Divine workmanship' which is 'created in Christ Jesus.'

True, they are exhibited here, only in miniature form. But is there not in the miniature style of painting a delicacy of bloom, an exquisiteness of finish, and a manner of touch which a large-sized picture is not so well fitted to convey? *In miniature form.*

Like the miniature on the walls, this short Epistle may not catch the eye so readily, and is more apt to be overlooked than others occupying greater space and prominence, while it will yield little if only scanned by a passing glance, but becomes richer and

The Epistle of St Paul to Philemon

sweeter in its suggestiveness the longer and more fondly we linger over it.

In the Book of Revelation, as in the Book of Nature, the tiniest leaf is a world within itself, often all the more wonderful that the perfection of finish is on so small and unpretending a scale.

Such a leaflet is this Epistle to Philemon.

II

THE STORY IN THE EPISTLE

THE story this Epistle bears in its bosom is not without its romance, truth in this case being 'stranger than fiction.' For a real life-drama lurks within it, conveyed to us in a few tender and broken accents.

We catch, indeed, but glimpses of the story A life-drama. through the loopholes of incidental expressions; but there is no lack of vividness or pathos in the tale they conjure up. It contains a double crisis. It is the story of a bondman enfranchised and of a soul redeemed.

We learn that in the town of Colossæ, away up among the remote highlands of Phrygia, in Asia Minor, there lived a worthy and wealthy man named Philemon.

He was a prominent and zealous Christian in his Philemon own neighbourhood, having been converted to the faith under the ministry of Paul ('Thou owest unto me thine own self,' he says, ver. 19), probably in the course of the Apostle's three years' work at Ephesus (Acts xix. 10; xx. 31), or on an occasion of his missionary journeys through Phrygia and Galatia (Acts xvi. 6; xviii. 23). The name 'Philemon' was borne by several Greek authors, and is otherwise not

The Epistle of St Paul to Philemon

unknown in the pages of classical literature. It has several associations with Phrygia. We hear of a Philemon (Aristophanes, *The Birds*, 762) that rendered himself the butt of public derision, centuries before this, for pretending to be a pure-blooded Athenian, though he was notoriously of *Phrygian* descent.

The name and its associations. But the most remarkable case, connecting this name with Phrygia, occurs in ancient mythical story. According to the legend (told with great beauty and simplicity by the poet Ovid, *Metamorphoses*, Book viii., 626, and retold by Dean Swift in his best style and in his best poem *Baucis and Philemon* 1707), Jupiter and Mercury paid a visit in disguise to a district in Phrygia, and besought hospitality in vain among the inhabitants. At last they come to a very humble hut, and are courteously received by its inmates, an aged couple, *Philemon* and his wife Baucis. Spreading out their lowly fare, they are startled to observe the wine-cup mysteriously replenish itself in the course of a meal; and, concluding their guests to be heavenly visitors, they hasten to catch their only remaining goose for a sacrifice. The bird, however, eludes all their efforts, and at last takes refuge with the strangers, who intimate that they accept the will for the deed and forbid its slaughter, though an example, they say, must be made of the impious and inhospitable neighbourhood. That the worthy pair may be preserved from the impending calamity, they are invited to go with their guests to the top of the neighbouring hill, whence they see the whole district

22

The Story in the Epistle

sink into a morass, except their own little hut, which A curious Legend. grows into a magnificent temple as they gaze. On Philemon being asked to express his fondest wish, he consults with Baucis, and they agree to desire that they be made keepers of the temple, and that neither might be spared to see the other's grave. Their desire was granted : and one morning as they were rehearsing the tale before the sacred fane, they found themselves growing into twin trees together, with time only to bid each other an affectionate farewell.

As a moral fable, intended to exalt the virtues of hospitality and conjugal love, this story stands far above the tone of ordinary mythological lore. Those who (like Abbé Huet) see in the better classical fictions perverted reminiscences of Old Testament history, recognise in the legend of Philemon and Baucis an echo of Abraham and Sarah entertaining angels unawares, with the attendant account of the overthrow of the cities of the plain. But the chief value of this story consists in the light it throws on Acts xiv. 11-13, where the barbarians of the very neighbourhood, as if recalling their local legends, and having strangely enough a priest and temple of Jupiter, reveal their acquaintance with such deities as Jupiter and Mercury, attributing to Barnabas and Paul their fitting characteristics. 'They called Acts xiv. 12. Barnabas, Jupiter, and Paul, Mercurius, because he was the chief speaker.'

The sketch the apostle gives of Philemon in the letter, reveals in no common degree some of the finest and most distinctive Christian graces. A

23

The Epistle of St Paul to Philemon

living faith in the Lord Jesus, showing itself practically in love and all good fruits (ver. 5); an active and public-spirited interest in the cause of Christ ('fellow-labourer,' the apostle calls him, ver. 1), and in the affairs of the Church (he accommodated a body of disciples with an apartment or worship-room in his house, ver. 2); generosity and liberality towards poor saints (ver. 7); a forgiving and placable temper (ver. 21); hospitableness and prayerfulness (ver. 22); these are some of the prominent and noble lineaments of Philemon's character, which made him worthy of the apostle's friendship, and which recommend him to our warmest respect.

Paul writes to him as a man in whom he had the utmost confidence, whose high principle and eminent saintliness were honourable to the Christian profession and a cause of thankfulness and comfort to his own heart (vers. 4-7).

We shall not, however, be surprised to hear of Philemon, notwithstanding all his Christian virtues and excellences, having slaves in his possession—that being the only form of service available in the condition of society as then constituted in Phrygia and elsewhere.

How Christianity stood towards slavery; how it regulated its working while looking askance upon it: how it tolerated it as the less of two grave evils, while seeking to countermine the sentiments on which it rested, and how it proposed to bring into operation those great principles of its own, which bore on slavery and kindred social questions—these

24

are elements that lend undying interest and value to the present Epistle.

Meanwhile, we need not feel shocked at Philemon employing slave-labour in his day, any more than at distinguished spiritually - minded Christians, now, being engaged in military pursuits, and many dubious walks of life, which the exigencies of the time may seem to render a painful but inevitable necessity, till society sweep forward into new and improved pathways. Philemon's household.

Nor, when we think of slavery as Philemon was familiar with it, are we to import into it those ideas which belong rather to the modern developments of the system. We are to picture it as a patriarchal arrangement rather than as a commercial speculation —a rough mode of dealing out justice rather than a conspiracy against the rights and well-being of men —a mode of supporting the dignity of rank rather than an attempted stigma on colour and race.

We are to conceive of Philemon as the master of an establishment of the Oriental kind such as the East still exhibits, according to manners that have remained stereotyped for centuries.

Such a system, where so little is regulated by any other law than long-standing usage, and where so much latitude is afforded to the holder of power, will be worked of course oppressively or tenderly, according to the disposition of each master. We shall therefore not err in concluding that Philemon would let his Christian spirit be felt in the treatment of his dependents, alleviating the hardships of their lot, while guarding against the capricious tyranny so

The Epistle of St Paul to Philemon

habitual to uncontrolled authority. It speaks volumes for his kindness that no ground for complaint is made in this letter, nor is the slightest whisper of cruelty heard against him.

Onesimus, a bondman.

Now, in this household of Philemon was a certain bondman, Onesimus (a common enough slave-name, meaning *serviceable*), whose story is the subject and occasion of this letter.   If it be asked, Was Onesimus a real *slave*?   the answer must be that he can hardly be thought of as anything else.   Some (like Albert Barnes), who desire to concede as little as possible to any supporters of slavery without conclusive evidence, would like to think of him as a servant by his own voluntary contract—contending that the word for *servant* applied to him in ver. 16 is not strictly and exclusively 'a slave.'   And certainly the Greek term in question is by no means so restricted as is our word slave (or sclave, from the Sclavonic peoples who, prior to the negro race, supplied Europe with victims of traffic), if by slave we mean one who may be bought and sold freely under the *absolute will* of the master.   Yet 'slave' is of very wide and varied applicability.

What kind of bondman

See Edwards's *Ancient Slavery*, pp. 8 and 94.

'*Bond*-servant' comes nearest the normal usage of the word, leaving indefinite the *nature* of the bonds, or the *way they were entered into*—the idea of servitude or bondage, however, being prominent, and not any service changeable at the liking of the servant. It is invariably the word for *bond* in such expressions as 'bond and free' (1 Cor. xii. 13 ; Eph. vi. 8).   It is the word for 'the *servants*' of the 'great house-holder,' in our Lord's parables, who are entrusted

26

with his goods, and who are yet liable to be *sold* with their children for *debt* (Matt. xviii. 25). Bond-servants might of course be stewards or overseers, or fill similar high posts of honour in an establishment like Philemon's, as well as be simple menials, while the *extent or severity* of the servitude varied according to the laws and usages of each neighbourhood. To understand the tenure of Philemon over Onesimus, we should keep in mind the stringency of Phrygian bondage. So notorious was this that Phrygian and slave were often used as interchangeable terms—Phrygia being a main source of supply to the slave-marts of the Roman Empire. What position Onesimus occupied as a bond-servant, whether he acted in some capacity of trust, or belonged to the lower grade of hand-labourer, or what place he filled, there is no clue to determine; though if we may judge from what Paul afterwards thought of him, it seems likely he was capable of a higher class of work.

We are told, however, he had proved but an unprofitable servant, and had certainly not submitted to the faith his master had adopted. From some cause or other, not precisely ascertainable, he resolved, as was common enough amongst his unfortunate class, to steal away from his bondage.

Many conjectures have been hazarded for his absconding. Was it that his nature revolted against his condition, and he wished to taste the sweets of freedom? or that he resented some disgrace or ignominious form of punishment? or dreaded the detection and penalty of some offence he had

Onesimus, the fugitive.

committed? Be this as it may, he directed his flight to the great metropolis of the world, amid whose vast populations he could best baffle pursuit and gain the ends he sought.

A skulking Victim and Outcast. The fact that he could traverse the long distance from Colossæ to Rome seems to point to his possession of funds very suspiciously acquired, to say the least. But these, like the most of ill-gotten moneys, must speedily have melted away; and we are constrained to think of the poor fugitive, the victim of his own folly, reduced to take refuge in the low slums of the city, and to herd with the outcast and depraved in their miserable haunts. We seem to see him skulking and prowling along the streets with the well-known aspect of the unfortunate or vagabond class: guilt in his looks, slouching hesitancy in his gait, haggard want in his face, and misery gnawing at his heart.

But there is hope even for such as he, however far down he has sunk. Rescue is nigh at hand.

Yet hope for him. Looking at the criminals and reprobates that infest the vile and infamous districts of Christian cities themselves, where the physical squalor is only equalled by the moral degradation, we grow at times almost painfully conscious of a paralysis of despair creeping over the heart while we sorrowfully inquire, ' *Can* these bones live?' and we only feel relieved when we read again, ' Thus saith the Lord God unto these bones, Behold, I will cause breath to enter into you, and ye shall live.'

Still when we think again of the vast hollow caverns of heathen corruption, and try to conceive

28

The Story in the Epistle

of souls coming forth out of these depositaries of the doubly dead, we imagine we might have cried, 'If the Lord open windows in heaven, then might such a thing be.'

But the Lord *had* opened windows in heaven: and a new message, clothed with power of life-breath, was being borne on the four winds into the very midst of the bleaching bone-heaps, and was pouring into multitudes, even more abandoned than Onesimus, the inspiration of a fresh faith and hope that raised them on their feet, a mighty and noble army.

The poor fugitive is led by a gracious Providence of God's Spirit to hear the gospel from the apostle's lips (under what circumstances we know not), and as he listens his conscience is stirred, his heart is melted, and he becomes a trophy of the cross. *Onesimus hears Paul's Gospel.*

'The wretch that once sang wildly, danced and laughed,
And sucked in dizzy madness with his draught,
Has wept a silent flood, reversed his ways,
Is sober, meek, is penitent, and prays ;
Abhors the craft he boasted of before,
And he that stole has learned to steal no more.'

We behold in him another prodigal in the interesting process of 'coming to himself.'

What the degradation and hardship of the swine-trough had been to the younger son in the parable ; what the prison in Babylon had been to Manasseh ; or what the shame and anguish of crucifixion to the dying malefactor—*that* had probably been the bitter disappointment and severe experiences of the streets of Rome to the weary wanderer Onesimus !

The Epistle of St Paul to Philemon

They had taught him to reflect on the error of his
ways, and opened up his heart, like a plough-share,
for the seed of the Word. He repents and believes
the gospel. He enters into *life*! And nobly does
he acquit himself in his new position.

How highly the apostle esteemed the convert,
and how greatly he valued the services of this 'son
in the faith,' Paul amply testifies throughout this
letter. To show the thoroughness of the change
which had passed on him, Onesimus is willing to
return to Philemon, cast himself on his master's
Christian generosity and forgiveness, and endeavour
to make reparation for the past. The apostle feels
the hardship of surrendering so valuable a helper;
but recognising the cardinal principle of gospel ethics,
that to make reparation as far as possible for any
mischief is a requisite of true repentance, he submits
to the personal sacrifice, and makes up his mind to
send Onesimus back.

But what care he takes to throw around his
returning convert, the broad ægis of gospel protection! He has no idea of Onesimus being hurried
off to his master again like a skulking or trembling
fugitive. He will take means to ensure that
Philemon, an old convert of his own, shall receive
and treat the bondman as verily a Christian friend
and brother. He waits a favourable opportunity for
restoring him in peace; and this occurs by the
occasion he has to send Tychicus on a mission to the
Churches in the valley of the Lycus (a tributary of
the more famous Mæander), of which this in Colossæ
was one.

The Story in the Epistle

He was the bearer of the public Epistle to that Church. 'All my state shall *Tychicus* declare unto you . . . whom I have sent unto you . . . with *Onesimus*, a faithful and beloved brother, who is *one of you. They* shall make known unto you all things which are done here ' (Coloss. iv. 7-9).

How admirable are these precautionary measures of the apostle on behalf of his protégé! He is solicitous that the slave shall not encounter the master by himself. He secures a mediator in Tychicus, while he certifies to the general Church the right of Onesimus to the full privileges of its membership.

Having done all this, has he not amply satisfied the requirements of the case? He thinks something may be done of a more private kind to conciliate Philemon. Hence this letter of personal friendship, which he puts at parting into the hands of Onesimus. That it secured not only a favourable reception for him, but his manumission in due time also, and his surrender to the public service of Christ, is generally understood. And it is difficult for us to conceive of any other result, with this exquisite letter before us. Onesimus, like Philemon himself, figures in ecclesiastical story as bishop and martyr. As usual, however, there is some confusion in the accounts. These traditional notices are often mere 'after-thoughts,' with little or no historical value, except in so far as they seem to confirm otherwise reasonable suppositions and inferences.

A Special Commendatory Letter.

There is thus a wheel within a wheel in the fortunes of Onesimus. He comes before us as a vindictive runaway; he disappears from our view,

A triumph of the Cross.

31

The Epistle of St Paul to Philemon

on the road to Colossæ, a brother beloved, with the highest credentials. The curtain rose on him as an alien at once from an earthly and a heavenly master, it drops on him as at peace with both.

The Gospel knows no despair. What a testimony to the grace and power of the gospel of Jesus Christ! The gospel alone knows no despair in the presence of the most appalling obstacles. It can rescue and elevate the lost and lapsed where other agencies must fail. It has found a way to the heart of the slave, as it already had done to the conscience of the master. It alone has learned to regard no case as hopeless, however deep the profligacy or abandoned the character; seeing in every outcast a real 'brother in the flesh' and a possible 'brother in the Lord' too ; and acting the part of the good Samaritan where culture and philosophy would pass coldly by on the other side, or leave the objects of their efforts as worthless and criminal as before.

Its message of mercy for each one. Here it lays its hand on a wretched outcast like Onesimus, and has neither spurned nor disowned him; neither mocked him in his straits nor left him in his misery and sin. For him, as for all, it has its message of mercy and its offer of grace and help. And so it goes on its way 'conquering and to conquer.' Not losing itself among the 'masses' or great aggregate of men, but dealing with them as individuals, it strives to bring near the Saviour to each, if haply each and all may be drawn near the Saviour, and be clasped in the embrace of that gracious Master 'whose service' alone is 'perfect freedom.'

32

III

SIGNIFICANCE AND VALUE OF THIS EPISTLE

APART from the interest which this letter awakens in the bondman Onesimus, it has supreme value and significance from a *social* point of view.

In its spirit and aims it is far ahead of 'all whereunto we have already attained' even yet, in our boasted progress of society—exhibiting principles which are capable of indefinite development, and, like an 'avant courier,' operating as a preparative and incitement to their own fuller realisation.

The letter is simply of priceless worth as a manual of domestic and social reform, continually beckoning human society to cast off those corruptions which endanger its interests or menace its very existence. For, like the prophetic oracles, it carries a 'burden' in its bosom—the burden of a momentous subject, or rather of a heterogeneous mass of subjects gathered up in the single term 'slavery'—a word of as wide and awful import as the dire one of 'war,' or others of kindred suggestiveness in the history of mankind —a word which Christian civilisation has taught us to regard as synonymous, at least in its grosser forms, with abject misery on the part of its victims, and remorseless cruelty on the part of its abettors.   For

A letter of priceless worth.

Its 'burden' is slavery.

The Epistle of St Paul to Philemon

of all systems of oppression it has lent chief countenance to the perilous calumny against the Divine Creator's honour, that 'man was made to mourn'; and of all social relationships it has afforded widest scope for the exercise of violent and flagitious passions most nearly approximating to the diabolical, and for the perpetration of the most inhuman atrocities.

And if it be a characteristic of abuses that they are singularly tenacious of existence, slavery has in this respect a bad pre-eminence. For among the obnoxious and malignant pests that have cursed the soil and poisoned the springs of social life, it has not only been notoriously virulent in its roots, but has developed itself with the most persistent vitality. Subdued in one form, it has cropped up in another— as endless in its disguises and as difficult to overpower as the fabled Proteus himself.

Yet *here* we have revealed to us how it *can* be mastered. For it is not too much to say that many as have been the books launched against slavery— treatises, tales, and orations—all that is best in anti-slavery laws and literature is anticipated here.

In this lies one chief value of the letter, that it not only illustrates Paul's *attitude* in regard to slavery, but it affords a picture of Christianity *at work* upon it, and with all the happy effects of a Christian spirit when brought into direct contact with its operation.

Here the whole system receives a death-blow, however long it may struggle in the lingering processes of dissolution. Here we have a prophecy

Reveals Paul's attitude to slavery.

34

Significance and Value of this Epistle

of its ultimate abolition. And 'blessed are our eyes, for they have seen' what many desired to see and saw not—sufficiently large instalments of slave emancipation on a gigantic scale as to afford ample security for universal disenthralment, and to augur in the eyes of even weak faith the final triumph of all principles that are akin to the blood-bought 'liberty wherewith Christ makes His people free.' And 'at length we seem to see the beginning of Vast the end. The rapid strides towards emancipation, modern results. during the present generation, are without a parallel in the history of the world. The abolition of slavery throughout the British Empire, at an enormous material sacrifice, is one of the greatest moral conquests which England has ever achieved. The liberation of twenty millions of serfs throughout the Russian dominions has thrown a halo of glory round the name of Alexander II. which no time can dim. The emancipation of the negro in the vast Republic of the New World was a victory not less important than either to the well-being of the human race. Thus within a period of little more than a quarter of a century this reproach of civilisation and humanity has been wiped out in the three greatest empires of the world. It is a fit sequel to these achievements that at length a well-directed attack should have been made on the central fortress of slavery and the slave trade, the interior of Africa. May we not venture to predict that in future ages this epoch will stand out in the history of mankind as the era of Lightfoot's liberation? If so, the Epistle to Philemon, as the *Introduction to the Epistle,* earliest prelude to these magnificent social victories, pp. 394, 395.

35

The Epistle of St Paul to Philemon

must be invested with more than common interest for our generation.'

With slavery as a practical matter of fact the primitive Christian Church was familiar enough; but it fell more particularly to the apostle Paul to grapple with the subject in its bearings on Christian life and the rights of Christ's people, continually crossing his path as it did when he was engaged in his great life-work of establishing Gentile Churches and settling their constitution.

How Paul handles the subject.

Nowhere, perhaps, does he exhibit a finer combination of 'mercy and truth, righteousness and peace,' than in the policy he pursued regarding this serious question.

That policy was not one of direct and violent denunciation, but of persuasive pressure. He knew well the nature and history of the evil with which he had to deal. Slavery was a most venerable and wide-spread institution, interwoven into the whole texture of society and affecting it in all its interests and relations. Dating its ancestry from beyond the flood, commanding universal suffrage in the ancient empires, and grown to colossal dimensions under Roman sway, it had come to be considered a necessity of common life. It was not one of those superficial growths which could be torn up at once. It had spread its roots too widely and deeply for that, in the soil of social existence. It ministered too successfully to the wants of human nature and to the stronger passions of men—to their lust of rule, their spirit of revenge and their sensual desires—to give way before occasional bursts of righteous

Gen. vi. 4, 11.

36

Significance and Value of this Epistle

indignation. It was one of those leviathans which 'laugh at the shaking of a spear.'

In many parts of the Roman Empire, as the apostle knew it, the slave population formed a vast majority. In the palmy days of Athens it is usually said that out of 421,000 inhabitants, no fewer than 400,000 were slaves. In Rome their number was often a subject of great uneasiness. Servile revolts and slave massacres were neither of them unfamiliar things, and the whole system was a matter of the most watchful attention and the most jealous legislation in the Senate. The great families possessed slaves by the thousand, four hundred being reckoned by Horace the appanage of a very modest household. *Sat.* i.

Old society based on slavery.

But their condition and treatment were more appalling than their numbers.

In the days of the apostle the Roman slave was absolutely at the mercy of the master—the law affording no protection against the most outrageous cruelty, and the power to inflict death privately by torture or otherwise not being taken away from the owner till the days of the Emperor Adrian (A.D. 117).

Slaves could hold no property, possess no rights, and form no legally recognisable relationships. They had no standing in any court of law, and if they were examined as witnesses, it was always under torture.

Fearful condition of slaves.

Many of them were doubtless well cared for— some of the better and more educated order, who filled the posts of stewards, tutors, and private secretaries, being valued at £700 or £800 (for one of this class as much as £5000 sterling is recorded to have been given)—but great masses of them lived

37

The Epistle of St Paul to Philemon

the life of the street-dog, being cast out to shift for themselves when too old or disabled for service, while the strongest and brawniest specimens were eagerly sought out for the gladiatorial and wild-beast fights in the amphitheatre.

For slight offences the penalty might be the lash, the chain, mutilation, starvation or crucifixion, at the caprice of the master. For breaking a crystal dish at a banquet given to Augustus by a wealthy citizen, one was condemned, in the master's passion, to be chopped to pieces and thrown to the lampreys of his fish-pond, which would have been done but for the interposition of the imperial guest himself. The runaway slave was liable to fearful tortures, but was usually branded in the face with a hot iron or condemned to wear a metal collar round the neck, with his name and offence engraven on it, and not seldom some insulting or irritating phrase, such as ' Seize me, for I abscond,' or ' Fetch me back to my owner.'

Annals of Tacitus, xiv. 42-45.
A tragic Illustration. Just about the time of Paul's entrance into Rome an awful tragedy had occurred which has often been pointed to as a fit but fearful illustration of the atrocities sanctioned by the Roman slave system.

Pedanius Secundus, a senator, prefect of the city, had been killed by one of his bondmen. According to an enactment passed in the reign of Augustus, about half a century before, it was provided that the whole body of slaves belonging to the master should in such a case be put to death along with the actual perpetrator of the deed, however innocent they might be of any complicity in his crime. The lives of no

38

fewer than four hundred men, women and children were to be sacrificed by this monstrous law.

The passions of the populace were roused, however, to prevent on this occasion the bloody holocaust; but after an anxious debate in the Senate it was resolved to enforce the law, and the fearful tragedy was completed. Bands of military were called out to overawe the mob, while the four hundred innocent victims were being publicly massacred in cold blood.

Such were some of the features and native results of that slave system with which the apostle was brought everywhere into contact. That his soul kindled against its evils, that he was inspired with compassion for its victims, and that he deeply pondered how best to deal with a subject that often wrung his heart with anguish, can alone explain the strong but subdued intensity of feeling that reigns through the pleadings of the present letter.

But whatever were his personal sensibilities and predilections, he was enabled, under Divine guidance, to take an enlightened and far-reaching view of the subject in all its bearings. He sees that if slavery in the world is ever to be effectually subdued, it must be by processes of conviction and through enlarged conceptions of human rights and responsibilities. *The Apostle's wise policy.*

A sound social system must be an outgrowth of moral and religious sentiments, that have to be unfolded to men's minds and enforced on their consciences before they can be realised in outward embodiment. This is a matter of time, and can only go hand in hand with other great and slow-moving works of change.

The Epistle of St Paul to Philemon

**His wise
Spirit and
Method.**

It has sometimes seemed to inconsiderate minds,
that because the apostle does not feel at liberty to
denounce or forbid slavery, and does not order every
Christian slaveholder to manumit his slaves, he so
far authorises the system. But this is seriously to
misunderstand the spirit and methods of Apostolic
Christianity. To draw up catalogues of organised
evils and label each according to its demerits would
have been a task no less worthless than Quixotic.

Suppose he had introduced the word slavery and
said, 'It is a wrong thing,' what endless questions
of casuistry would have sprung up as to what is
slavery! Is it simply buying and selling men? Is
serfdom or predial vassalage or villeinage to be held
therefore as fully sanctioned, because not covered by
the apostle's dictum? Or if a man take advantage
of the misfortunes of a fellow-man, and yoke him to
crushing and ill-requited toil for his daily bread, is
there no essence of slave-making in that?

**He goes to
root of
Evil.**

The apostle is well aware that slavery in its whole
length and breadth could never fall, unless the
grounds and reasons of the thing be dealt with, and
not the mere outward thing itself with a few of its
attendant circumstances.

The gospel never sets forth mere legal formulæ,
which can easily be evaded by some subtlety. It
commits itself to no abstract or hard and fast
deliverances about particular or constantly fluctuating
abuses; its mission is to human nature itself—the
soil out of which all evils grow.

Slavery in Paul's view is not an *institution* so
much as a *subtle spirit*, whose evil genius may be

40

Significance and Value of this Epistle

largely at work, even where its grosser usages have passed away.

Thus in our own more advanced social arrangements, when trafficking in human flesh and blood has been outgrown, at least in its more disgusting forms, we should be sadly mistaken to suppose there are no slaveries still in the midst of us. And who does not feel that if society is to escape from these, it must make strides in advance, compared with which its previous attainments are as the stumblings of childhood? Elevated though we have been into another atmosphere altogether from the stifling horrors of old Rome, or of mediæval and feudal Europe, we must pass up into much higher reaches before we can be said to enjoy in our social relations that full and pure and perfect freedom which this letter breathes.

Slavery is only one of many outward arrangements **No abstract** with all of which the apostle has to deal in the same **denunciation** way, so as to lay the axe effectually at their root. **suffices.**

If he had singled out social slavery for specific attack, it might have seemed as if that were the chief or only evil needing to be subverted. Buying and selling men is not the solitary bondage. Does not war involve military slavery? What is autocratic despotism but political slavery? Persecuting and intolerant principles mean ecclesiastical slavery; and reckless speculation and competition involve multitudes in the thraldom of a commercial form of slavery.

Yet the apostle never dreams of saying 'War is wrong,' or 'You must not be an autocrat,' or

41

The Epistle of St Paul to Philemon

'Despotism is wrong.' He knew the folly of merely saying 'Abolish war,' 'Manumit your slaves,' 'Never be a soldier,' 'Never own allegiance to a despot.'

A new Spirit to be evoked. Christianity is not a dictatorial tyranny, stripping men of their solemn responsibilities. While inculcating principles of the boldest sweep and the keenest incisiveness, it lays their special application in large measure on those who receive them, so as both to train and test their spiritual disposition and aptitude.

Alike by the truths it teaches, the precepts it enforces, and the sentiments it creates, the gospel annihilates the grounds on which all slavery rests, and thereby morally abolishes and subverts its operation, though it cannot abrogate and annul, like a civil power, the external relations of life over which that civil power is ordained by God to have immediate control.

If, therefore, Onesimus is to be emancipated, it cannot be done by apostolic fiat, but by the force of sacred convictions in Philemon's own breast.

No Countenance to Anarchy. Had the apostle said to the masters, 'You must at once manumit your slaves,' he would have put himself into a hopelessly false position, intruding into the sphere of the civil ruler, and usurping magisterial functions. To unfurl the standard of immediate and divinely enjoined 'abolition,' would have been for the apostle to chain Christianity *authoritatively* to the demons of revenge, violence and uncontrollable fury. For many of the slave population would have hailed the new faith as the signal and rallying-ground for raising the standard of revolt and armed resistance against their masters, under the sanction of a Divine commission.

The apostle is careful to lend no countenance to such wild projects. Think of the inconsistency of a Christian apostle invoking the spirit of war in its worst horrors in order to put down by force the mere *external evils* of slavery! For the most successful war of emancipation can never eradicate the power and spirit of slavery, if not otherwise prepared for by ripened conviction and principle; and Christianity, in upholding the sentiments of universal justice and benevolence, can never appear as the patron of anarchy and bloodshed.

Slavery is a mixed question, domestic, social and political, and is therefore far too intricate and complicated to be summarily handled on exclusively religious grounds. If, therefore, Paul does not wander out of his sacred province by denouncing slave-holding as a crime, it is because he is prepared to go so much further, and use much more effective methods for subverting the curse. *Slavery a mixed Question.*

It is easy to rail at giant abuses and hurl against them great sounding words of fury signifying nothing; but it is another thing to lay down a base of operations for securing effective triumphs.

Here is a giant fortress, too strong and too well garrisoned to be taken by storm, all at once. Paul therefore approaches it by processes of sapping and mining, content to burrow away beneath its lowest foundations silently, so that they may at last sink by their own weight and crumble into dust. He leaves them a prey to such beneficently explosive *Processes of Sapping and Mining*

43

forces as he here prepares, so that 'one stone may not be left upon another, that shall not be thrown down.' For slavery is not so much a sin or evil in itself, as a result of other sins and evils. It is *these* that must be first dealt with.

There are modes of slavery that are not abstractly unjustifiable. If by slavery be meant depriving a man of his natural liberty, there are occasions when this may and must be done. A prisoner is a slave, bound to toil without reward. The malefactor may manifestly forfeit his full possession of himself; and others may acquire a proprietary right in him for a time. And if a man may sell his *services*, who will deny that to restrain him from selling *himself* is a curtailment of his liberty of action, that must be based on some other ground than the inherent sinfulness of the act itself?

The real ground for issuing laws against slavery is not so much the essential wickedness of the relationship itself, as the practical impossibility of separating from it certain classes of evil and wickedness intolerable to Christianised minds, and disastrous to the best interests of human life.

Various degrees of servile Labour.

But there are stages of society where some kinds of slavery may be the most effective punishment of crime, or be preventive of worse evils than itself, or be a suitable exponent of the principles of justice. These may no doubt be very exceptional eventualities; but the fact that there are such cases at all is itself a sufficient reason why the apostle does not proceed against slavery by abstract deliverances or direct pronouncement. On this account he tolerates

44

Significance and Value of this Epistle

the evil without concealing his aversion to it; he provides regulations and arrangements necessary alike for master and bondman, without failing to show his preference for 'a more excellent way' of social existence; and while he will not inveigle slaves into Christianity by holding out to them the tempting bait of immediate freedom, he calls on them to burst their fetters by developing those graces and habits which would render the usages of slavery a moral impossibility, and so to realise that 'in Christ there is neither bond nor free.'

The special feature of the present letter is that in it Paul deals not with the slave but with the master; and his grand object is to set before Philemon the *right point of view* from which he must learn henceforward to regard Onesimus. His main concern is not about the *external forms* of the relationship of master and bondman, but *the inner spirit* that should pervade them. _{The right point of view.}

The apostle therefore strives to inoculate Philemon within certain principles of a subtle and far-reaching character, which are partly of immediate application, but chiefly of progressive force and virtue as men are able to receive them.

He says, for example, First: That all men, whether slaves or masters, are to be regarded as naturally brethren. No human being is to be treated, therefore, as a brute beast, still less as a chattel; but every man, by virtue of the very nature he wears, as a 'brother in the flesh.' _{Four far-reaching principles.}

Secondly: All Christians, whatever their social relations, are to view one another as 'brethren in the

45

The Epistle of St Paul to Philemon

Lord'—belonging all to the same order in Christ, whatever variety of status or worth each may hold in it.

Thirdly: The Christian communion, or organised fellowship, is to be regarded as the outward sign and seal of these facts, giving room and scope for their practical manifestation.

And finally: While Paul lays down no injunction to which Philemon must adhere, he makes no secret of his own predilections. Bond-service is an obnoxious idea to his mind. He would feel uncomfortable in employing it. 'Not of necessity, but willingly' (ver. 14), is the motto of the only service he would reckon worth having for himself, or fit to be called *true* service.

Such are some of the more prominent teachings of this letter. The apostle knows well he need have no misgivings regarding the reception and treatment of Onesimus, if only Philemon can be persuaded to adopt and act on them. This would be to secure much more than manumission for the bondman. It would Christianise, and therefore entirely modify, the whole spirit of the relationship, and finally subvert every system of social life which would be out of harmony with such fundamental principles.

Let these hardy growths once take root in the soil of human nature, and they will eventually effect a thorough clearance from the face of the earth of many a strange and noxious plant that cannot otherwise be got rid of. For there are weeds that can never be extirpated by merely pulling at them. To try to tear them up by force is but to leave endless fibres in the ground for worse and wider development. Such stubborn pests must be choked down by the overmastering power of wholesome plants, if they are to be thoroughly exterminated and leave no other trace behind them than a salutary remembrance of their odiousness.

This is the policy of 'slow but sure' which has **Slow work** commended itself to universal experience as the best **of change.** and wisest for difficult and tentative measures. We find it recommended in the proverbial philosophy of most nations — even the most determined and energetic. The active-spirited Roman said, 'Festina lente,' which the Italian echoes in his 'Chi va piano, va sano,' and the resolute German in his, 'Eile mit Weile'; while our own practical mind has taught us 'the greater hurry, the less speed.' Such a policy wisely and steadily applied will ever prove the most effectual antidote to every arrangement by which

> 'The natural bond of brotherhood
> Is severed as the flax, that falls asunder
> At the touch of fire,'

as well as to all those immoral feelings and desires which lend poignancy to the bitter charge:

> 'Man's inhumanity to man
> Makes countless thousands mourn.'

It is no more possible for the traffic and usages of **Slavery** slavery to subsist under the free action of the prin- **versus** ciples which the apostle here enunciates, than for **Christianity.** snow to remain on the housetops before the thaw that undermines it in trickling streams.

How can men make merchandise of those whom

The Epistle of St Paul to Philemon

yet they acknowledge to be at once brethren in the flesh and in the Lord? How can Christian men hold their fellows in bondage, and yet admit them to all the rights and privileges of Church membership and communion in the Lord? They may do it wilfully or ignorantly, but it is impossible to do it consistently.

Paul hastens to call the slave Onesimus 'my own son,' my very heart, a brother beloved, a fellow communicant, to be received as myself. Let Philemon look at his bondman *thus*, and while it is not the apostle's place and province to insist on emancipation, yet if something even better than this do not follow, it could only be because the master failed to appreciate, or carry out to their legitimate conclusion, the suggestive lessons of this Epistle.

It were uncharitable in us to think so ill of Philemon.

IV

SPIRIT OF THE EPISTLE

WHILE much of the attractiveness of this letter depends on the interest it awakens in us towards Philemon and Onesimus, its chief value of a personal kind is derived from the light it sheds on the Christian spirit displayed by the apostle himself. *Private Letters reveal Character.*

The features of his renewed nature are too vividly presented not to have special prominence assigned them in any exposition of the Epistle. We cannot too much extol, or feel too powerfully drawn to that great character, whose excellences this letter so illustriously exemplifies.

As a rule, we may learn more accurately the real qualities of a man from his private or familiar letters than from his more public correspondence. He more thoroughly reveals himself in the free and easy unbendings of friendly intercourse than in the utterances of official communication. Many a high reputation has been swamped by the posthumous publication of familiar correspondence, or the detailed account of the privacies of life.

The fact that this familiar letter is in our hands, and that Paul preserves in it the same tone and writes precisely in the same strain he uses elsewhere, is one of those incidental circumstances that enable *This reveals Christ in Paul.*

The Epistle of St Paul to Philemon

us to realise the intense *unity* of his character, his entire and absolute *self-consistency*. He is everywhere the same devout, humble, earnest, holy, and loving man, with the same Christian dispositions and qualities pervading all his public and private life and work.

But the commentator would prove recreant to the apostle's own mind were he to glorify Paul personally, and not rather *Christ in Paul*. This would be to forget his own key to that better self of which he says, '*I live, yet not I, but Christ liveth in me.*'

It is from this point of view we would regard the letter, as ' magnifying the grace of the Lord Jesus ' in all the beautiful commingling of those various traits of Christian character to which our attention is drawn.

Jonathan Edwards has a sermon entitled ' The excellency of Jesus Christ.' The text is Rev. v. 5 and 6 : ' Behold, the *Lion* of the tribe of Juda. . . . And I beheld, and lo . . . a *Lamb* as it had been slain.'

Conjunction of diverse Excellences. Fastening on the two names of *Lion* and *Lamb*, as representing our Lord, the preacher proceeds with his usual felicity and force to show ' that there is an admirable conjunction of diverse excellences in Jesus Christ,' such as majesty and meekness, glory and humiliation, justice and graciousness, terribleness and tenderness ; in short, the diverse excellences typified in the opposite qualities of two such creatures as the lion and the lamb.

Now it is with the servant in some measure as with the Master.

50

Spirit of the Epistle

The present Epistle shows how in this respect Paul 'followed the Lord wholly,' even although 'afar off.'

His position as mediator between Philemon and Onesimus afforded a favourable opportunity for illustrating this special phase of the Christlike spirit, as the clasp that binds together the hemispheres of a full-orbed perfectness and the reconciler of opposite excellences that are too often divorced and too easily regarded as all but incompatible in the same individual. Opposite graces in the Case.

He had confessedly a delicate cause to plead, and stood in such a delicate relation to both the parties at variance. He has to conciliate Philemon without humiliating Onesimus. He has to commend the wrong-doer without extenuating his offence. He has to balance the claims of justice and mercy— overcoming the prejudices of the master, yet securing the rights and privileges of the bondman as a brother beloved in Christ.

Yet it has been felt by every competent judge with what exquisite grace and tact he handles the fragile case, and with what a complete mastery he has triumphed over its hazards.

This could only be by bringing into play very diverse excellences indeed.

There is a famous letter of classic literature by the younger Pliny, one of the most perfect adepts in this form of composition, which, on account of its having been called forth in somewhat similar circumstances, has been usually associated with this of Paul to Philemon. We will let it speak for itself.

51

The Epistle of St Paul to Philemon

'CAIUS PLINY TO SABINIANUS. GREETING.

Similar
Letter by
Pliny.

'Your freedman, against whom you had declared
yourself incensed, came to me, and having cast
himself at my feet, he clung to them as if at your
own. He wept much, and much he did entreat:
much also he was silent; in short, he convinced me
of his penitence. I verily believe him changed for
the better, because he is sensible of having done
wrong. I know you are angry, and that you have
good ground to be angry I also know; but the glory
of clemency is greatest when the cause for anger is
the most just. You have loved the man, and I hope
you will love him: meanwhile it is enough that you
permit yourself to be entreated. It will be right
enough for you to be angry again, should he deserve
it: and you will be so with greater propriety, after
having been overcome by entreaty.

'Remit something on account of his youth, remit
something on account of his tears, remit a little out
of regard to your own kindliness: torture him not,
lest you torture also yourself. For it is self-torture
when one so gentle as you gets angry.

'I fear lest I may seem not to ask, but to exact,
if I were to add my own to his prayers. Yet I will
do so, all the more fully and freely that I have been
sharply and severely reproving him, having strictly
threatened never hereafter to intercede. This to him
whom it was well to alarm, but not the same to
you. For perhaps I shall ask again, and again
obtain: let it only be such as may become me to ask
and you to grant. Farewell.'

52

Spirit of the Epistle

This appeal was successful, as we learn from a subsequent letter as follows :

'CAIUS PLINY TO HIS FRIEND SABINIANUS. HEALTH.

'You have done well in having taken back to your house, to your favourable regard, the freedman (the freedman that had aforetime been dear to you) in compliance with the solicitations of my letter. This will afford gratification to yourself: it certainly does so to me—inasmuch as, in the first place, I see that you are governable in your anger ; and, in the next place, you attach so much weight to myself as either to submit to my authority or yield to my entreaties. I therefore both compliment and thank you, while at the same time I advise you for the future to be ever ready to show yourself placable towards the faults of your domestics, even though there be no one to turn aside your anger. Farewell.'

This is certainly very beautiful writing, and very The effective in its pleading, but, according to the verdict Contrast. of critical judges, not to be compared with this Epistle to Philemon even in some of those graces of rhetorical expression in which the Roman writer was a master, much less in those diviner qualities of head and heart wherein he is so plainly and painfully deficient. The one is the letter of a kindly and polished, but withal a frigid *littérateur* ; the other is the letter of an earnestly yearning and tender-hearted Christian apostle, whose rapid and condensed style is the fit exponent of his exalted thoughts and emotions.

The Epistle of St Paul to Philemon

What a play we have here of contrary excellences in happy harmony, like the varied features of a countenance mingling together into one settled cast of expression! What an illustration of the paradoxes of Christian love!

As in Paul's great eulogium on the spirit of charity, this one fundamental grace is seen to transform itself into various others—such as *humility*, for 'charity vaunteth not itself, is not puffed up': *patience*, for 'it is not easily provoked': *mercifulness*, for 'it suffereth long and is kind': *unselfishness*, 'for it seeketh not its own':—thus the list of its virtues runs forward—so we see Paul's own love at work in this letter (which is really a practical commentary by himself on 1 Cor. xiii.) under many various forms, like—

> 'Friendship which once determined never swerves,
> Weighs ere it trusts, but weighs not ere it serves ;
> And soft-eyed peace, and intercession bland ;
> And melting tenderness with open hand ;
> And confidence, believing and believed ;
> And honest faithfulness which ne'er deceived ;
> And pity stretching out ere want can speak,
> To wipe the tear which stains affliction's cheek.'

'This Epistle sheweth' (to use the words of Luther's oft-quoted preface), 'a right noble example of lovely Christian love. Here we see how St Paul layeth himself out for poor Onesimus, and with all his means pleadeth his cause with his master, and so setteth himself as if he were Onesimus, and had himself done wrong to Philemon. . . . Even as Christ did for us with God the Father, thus also doth St

Spirit of the Epistle

Paul for Onesimus with Philemon. . . . For we are all, to my thinking, *His* Onesimuses.'

And as the apostle has thus to 'lay his hand upon both,' and harmonise very conflicting interests, nothing but the spirit of this lovely Christian love could avail to melt down the elements of hardness and antagonism, and mould them into unison. For what is this Christian love but the bond of perfectness—the spirit that mediates among the numberless graces and excellences of the higher nature—the ring with which we should wed each virtue to its counterpart?

How admirable is the conjunction of opposite elements here!   Would we have an example of *dignity* and *humility*? we need only turn to verses 8 and 9: 'Though I might be much bold in Christ to *enjoin*, . . . yet for love's sake I rather *beseech*:' or of *justice* and *generosity*, we need only read verses 18, 19: 'If he hath wronged thee, or oweth thee ought, put that on mine account: . . . albeit I do not say to thee how thou owest unto me even thine own self besides.'

And so he mingles, by the same spirit, *zeal* with *prudence, gentleness* with *faithfulness*, having all the confidingness of a childlike simplicity with all the circumspection of a sage-like wisdom. He feels there is a need to be, and so he is at pains to be, both 'wise as the serpent, yet harmless as the dove,' not allowing any single element to become exaggerated or over-charged. Love includes all Excellences.

What care he manifests to avoid one-sidedness, and to counteract in others so common a failing! Beautifully balances them.

55

The Epistle of St Paul to Philemon

This may be gathered from the constant recurrence of qualifying turns of thought and expression. We may illustrate this very noticeable feature of the Epistle, from the remarkable frequency of certain modifying particles like 'but' which occurs oftener, in verses 11-16 than in any other six verses of Scripture, and similar qualifying phraseology. 'Though having boldness to enjoin, *yet*'; 'in times past unprofitable to thee, *but*'; 'whom I would have retained, *but*'; 'receive him as myself, *but if.*' With what niceness the apostle holds throughout 'the *balances* of the sanctuary!' So, if he beseech Philemon to forego all vindictive feelings, it is not at the expense of truth and righteousness; and if he ask Onesimus to return and make amends to the master, it is not at the sacrifice of his own moral rights and Christian dignity.

There is such a tendency in even regenerate human nature to rack or maim, as on a bed of Procrustes, the fair form of Christian grace and sentiment, or change it into caricature! Men no sooner get hold of something that is unmistakably good, than they begin to pull it out strongly in one direction, and forget to do so on its other side.

Hateful Falsity of Extremes. This hateful 'falsehood of extremes' is a fertile source of corruption and error in doctrinal, experimental, and practical Christianity. Not that we need deprecate extremes in themselves, if only we guard against those that are one-handed. We can afford to be extreme in any one right direction, if only we are extreme in the correspondingly opposite right direction. We may be 'wise as the serpent,'

56

Spirit of the Epistle

provided we be equally careful to be 'harmless as the dove,' each being incomplete without the other; the serpent's wisdom would by itself be cunning, and the dove's harmlessness mere imbecility.

Some of the old moralities would have said, 'Strike a medium'; but Christ says, 'Be both combined: bring each extreme of good to its relative extreme, and blend them into one.'

For lack of this, what tumours and excrescences may grow! Zeal for God may easily lapse into bigotry or persecution, if not balanced by humanity: conscientiousness sink into miserable scrupulosity and casuistry, if not informed by intelligent conviction: tenderness of heart may be extinguished under a perverse plea of integrity: and even the sentiments of devotion may breed morbid fancies and noxious superstitions, unless regulated by the exercise of the active virtues. ^{Danger of One-sidedness.}

Against evils of such a nature the present Epistle is fitted to act as a safeguard, by exhibiting the beauty of a full-orbed and symmetrical development of Christian love—the reflection of the very glory of the cross of Christ, where the spirit of reconciliation operates on a boundless scale, and where no less 'mercy and truth meet together, righteousness and peace embrace each other.'

TRANSLATION AND PARAPHRASE

TRANSLATION[1]

(The text followed is that of the Hexaglot, edited by E. R. De Levante. Lond. 1876.)

1. PAUL, a prisoner of Jesus Christ, and Timothy[2] the brother, to Philemon the beloved, and our fellow-labourer, **Address and Salutations.**

2. And to Apphia the sister,[3] and to Archippus our fellow-soldier, and to the Church in thy house:

3. Grace be to you, and peace, from God our Father, and the Lord Jesus Christ.

4. I thank my God always,[4] making mention of thee in my prayers,

[1] Altered from the Common Version of 1611 as slightly as possible. The Epistle divides itself naturally into four parts: The Inscription and Salutation, verses 1-3; The Exordium or Prologue, verses 4-7; The Body of the Letter, verses 8-22; and the Conclusion, verses 23-25.

[2] *The* brother, *i.e.*, who is so well known to yourself and others. Nothing is lost by attaching full force and value to the pronouns, articles, and minor parts of speech as employed by the apostle. One main evidence, for example, of his own authorship of this Epistle (apart from Timothy) depends on his use of the first person *singular* all through, except in the sentences of salutation.

[3] Apphia *the sister* (instead of *the beloved*) is probably the more correct reading. The text of this Epistle is singularly pure, the variations in the chief manuscripts being very few and unimportant.

[4] Whether 'always' should be attached to the first or the second clause—to the *thanks* or the *prayers*—is of little moment: the best interpreters join it as above. The whole Exordium, verses 4-7, is

The Epistle of St Paul to Philemon

The
Prologue
or
Exordium.
5. Hearing of thy love and faith, which thou hast toward the Lord Jesus, and unto all the saints ;

6. That the fellowship of thy faith may become effectual, in the knowledge of everything good that is in us,[1] unto Christ Jesus.

7. For I had[2] much joy and consolation in thy love, because the hearts of the saints have been refreshed by thee, brother.

The body of
the letter.
8. Wherefore, though having much confidence[3] in Christ to enjoin on thee what is becoming,[4]

9. Yet, for love's sake, I beseech rather—being such an one,[5] (I do) as Paul, an old man,[6] and now also a prisoner of Jesus Christ,

10. Beseech thee for my child, whom I have begotten in my bonds, Onesimus ;[7]

11. Who in time past was to thee unprofitable, but now is profitable to thee and to me :

an intricate and difficult passage. Explanations will be found in their proper place.

[1] The right reading is not *in you*, but *in us ;* that is, in *us Christians,* us of the same fellowship as thyself.

[2] ' I had ' is much better attested than either ' *we* have,' or ' *we* had.'

[3] Or a consciousness of authority in Christ.

[4] Or Christianly befitting : ' convenient ' (Authorised Version), in the older sense of being *morally proper.*

[5] This refers to what goes before. Invested as I am with authority, yet ready on any occasion to waive its rights, out of loving considerations.

[6] Instead of ' *an old man,*' some would render ' *an ambassador.*'

[7] The name should not come in earlier than this. Paul delays mentioning it as long as possible. Onesimus means *profitable.* Note how genially Paul alludes to this.

Translation

12. Whom I have sent back to thee; HIM (receive as myself),[1] that is, mine own flesh,[2]

13. Whom I would have retained with me, that in thy stead he might minister unto me in the bonds of the gospel:

14. But without thine assent would I do nothing; that thy service[3] should not be as it were of necessity, but willingly.

15. For perhaps[4] to this end he departed for a season, that thou shouldest receive him to thyself for ever; Explanations, Arguments, and Appeals.

16. No longer as a bondman, but above a bondman, a brother beloved, especially to me, but how much more to thee, both in the flesh, and in the Lord:

17. If thou countest me therefore a partner,[5] receive him as myself.

18. But if he wronged thee in any respect, or oweth aught, put that to mine account;

19. I, Paul, have written it with mine own hand,

[1] There is no verb here in the original. An expression must therefore be borrowed by anticipation from verse 17, where the sense finds its completion.

[2] ' Mine own *bowels*,' a strong metaphor common to many languages as a term of affection—one very near and dear to me.

[3] Literally, 'that thy good,' or, as the earlier versions put it, 'that the good thou doest;' meaning, that the benefit thou wouldst render me.

[4] Not ' perhaps he departed '—he *did* actually depart: but ' he departed, perhaps that thou mightest get him fully back to thyself in *spiritual* and therefore *eternal* bonds.'

[5] That is to say, a member in Christian communion with thyself—a partaker of all the rights and privileges of a common fellowship in Christ.

63

The Epistle of St Paul to Philemon

I will repay: so that I may not say to thee that thou owest to me even thine own self besides.[1]

20. Yea, brother, may I have joy[2] of thee in the Lord: refresh my heart in Christ.[3]

21. Having confidence in thy obedience I have written to thee, knowing that thou wilt also do more than I say.

22. But at the same time be preparing[4] also a lodging for me: for I am hoping that through your prayers I shall be given unto you.

Closing Words.
23. There saluteth thee Epaphras, my fellow-prisoner in Christ Jesus,

24. Mark, Aristarchus, Demas, Luke, my fellow-labourers.

25. The grace of our Lord Jesus Christ be with your spirit. [Amen.][5]

---

[1] Besides what you owe me for Onesimus: you are still in my debt.

[2] Rather more literally, 'May I get *profit* of thee'; there being distinctly another allusion to the meaning of 'Onesimus'; and the '*I*' is emphatic.

[3] 'In Christ' is now adopted universally as the correct reading, and not 'in the Lord,' repeated from the previous clause.

[4] The *present* imperative tense indicates the hope of an immediate release: and the 'I am hoping' expresses not merely a wish, but a reasonable expectation.

[5] *Amen* is a liturgical word, and forms no part of the original text. The usual subscription, 'Written from Rome to Philemon, by Onesimus, a servant,' is only a traditional note without authority. It is exceedingly improbable that Paul would use Onesimus in writing a letter so nearly concerning himself. Epaphras would more likely be the penman in the present instance, if the apostle called in the aid of an amanuensis at all.

A FAMILIAR PARAPHRASE

PREFATORY EXPLANATION

THE purpose of a paraphrase is to secure certain objects which cannot be so well gained by the most perfect translation, just as the faithful translation has valuable advantages above a paraphrase.

Difference between Paraphrase and Translation.

A translation should convey *exactly*, a paraphrase should EXPRESS and IMPRESS *fully*, the meaning of an author. Idiomatic precision should characterise the one, faithful expansion the other.

Now there are such differences between the genius of the classical and the modern tongues as to render a paraphrase often needful, in order to produce on us the same strength of effect as was made on the original reader. The ancients were concise writers. Their tendency was to use methods of condensation, on account of the scarcity of writing material. As readers they were slow and careful, catching more in less space than we moderns usually do.

Translations do not, therefore, awaken readily the same flow of thought and suggestion. This can be best gained by the use of those expanded methods of writing to which the modern eye is more accustomed. A translation, moreover, often sounds foreign and less familiar in its accents. Its very brevity of utterance renders its meaning sometimes obscure. To

E   65

The Epistle of St Paul to Philemon

many ordinary readers, how full must this Epistle appear of hallowed, it may be, yet rather hazy expressions!

Hence the service that may be rendered by free or even colloquial paraphrases of many parts of Scripture —a service of which this Epistle to Philemon stands in especial need, as being so compressed and rapid in its style, and of which it peculiarly admits, as being a private letter with much of the free and familiar about it. There are paraphrases, more or less valuable, by Doddridge, Benson, Wells, and Bishop Shuttleworth; while Steele (in his *Christian Hero*) has thrown the Epistle into the form of a brief eighteenth-century complimentary letter; as follows:

'SIR,

An Eighteenth Century Paraphrase.

'It is with the deepest satisfaction that I every day hear you commended, for your generous behaviour to all of that faith, in the articles of which I had the honour and happiness to initiate you; for which, though I might presume to an authority to oblige your compliance in a request I am going to make to you, yet choose I rather to apply myself to you as a friend than an apostle, for with a man of your great temper, I know I need not a more powerful pretence than that of my age and imprisonment. Yet it is not my petition for myself, but in behalf of the bearer, your servant Onesimus, who has robbed you, and ran away from you: what he has defrauded you of I will be answerable for, this shall be a demand upon me; not to say that you owe me your very self: I called him your servant, but he is now also to be

66

A Familiar Paraphrase

regarded by you in a greater relation, even that of your fellow-Christian : for I esteem him a son of mine as much as yourself; nay, methinks it is a certain peculiar endearment of him to me, that I had the happiness of gaining him in my confinement. I beseech you to receive him, and think it an act of Providence that he went away from you for a season, to return more improved for your service for ever.'

PAUL TO PHILEMON

I am at present a prisoner in bonds for the sake of **Greetings.** Jesus Christ. And as Timothy (the brother who is now with me) desires to join in the representations of this letter, I associate him with myself in saluting thee, Philemon, our beloved common friend and fellow-labourer in the gospel. We greet also (thy wife) our sister Apphia; Archippus (your son), our fellow-soldier in Christ; and the whole body of the brethren who meet together as a church in thy house. May the blessings of grace and peace be vouchsafed to you all from God our Father and the Lord Jesus Christ!

As regards thyself personally, I thank my God for the delightful tidings I have been hearing of thy faith toward the Lord Jesus, and thy love to all His saints.

I have therefore been remembering you [1] continu- **Prayers.**

[1] To take away the stiffness of using the singular pronoun of the second person, we here glide into the ordinary plural form, although it must be understood that it is *Philemon alone* who continues to be addressed in the letter—the others not being referred to again till about the very conclusion.

The Epistle of St Paul to Philemon

ally in my prayers, and have been led, through certain events connected with yourself at this time, very especially to pray that the Christian fellowship established among us, and to which you belong by virtue of your faith, may show its practical efficiency by your being led into happy accord with ourselves, so that you may thoroughly know, and firmly approve of, all the good that we possess in Christ, to the promotion of *His* honour, and the exaltation of *His* name.

Thanks. Meanwhile, it has gratified me exceedingly, and cheered me in my bonds, to learn how much this fellowship has already availed with you; and I thank God for the joy and comfort I have felt from your sympathy and kindness towards many of the poor and distressed Christian saints. It refreshes *my* heart to hear of *their* hearts being refreshed by your goodness to them, my dear brother. Trusting, then, to your Christian generosity, and assured that you will at all times give free scope to these admirable traits of Christian character for which you are well known, I would bring under your notice the following case of a poor saint whom I desire to commend to your regard.

Appeals. I do not mean to appeal at present to my apostolic authority, for, though I might use the language of command, as I have a right to do in all matters of faith and practice, I prefer, out of respect to the claims and dictates of love, simply to beseech and entreat you at this time as a Christian friend. I would not challenge your obedience, where the whole virtue of the action consists, not in your complying with any injunction of mine, but in cherishing

68

A Familiar Paraphrase

and manifesting such feelings as the occasion may show to be right and fit.

Being then such a one as Paul, growing an old man, and also now a sufferer in bonds for Christ's sake, I wish to beseech you on behalf of a *protégé* of my own, whom I have won to Christ in the course of my prison labours. It is—let me mention the name—my own true child in the faith, Onesimus, once far enough, I know, from verifying such a name [Onesimus, the Serviceable]. But what tidings I bring to you about him! 'Can anything be too hard for the Lord?' He is a true Onesimus now, and he has proved eminently serviceable to me. He will, I doubt not, prove equally so to yourself. For I am sending him back to you, dear as he is to me and hard to part with.

I love and esteem him as my own soul, and I feel, Commen-
in letting him go, as if my very self were being dations.
wrenched asunder. Fain could I keep him, well-fitted as I think him to take your place in discharging any offices which you might desire to do me. But I would not have the appearance of extorting benefits, and this would look like engaging you without your own consent, a form of enforced service I should not feel free to avail myself of.

But apart from this, I have wished him to return, for in that he has been separated from you for a time, who knows but it was for the express purpose that you might get him back in different bonds altogether? For I would have you look at the matter in the light of the actual events, as they have come about in Divine Providence.

69

The Epistle of St Paul to Philemon

Onesimus is not quite the same sort of being you formerly possessed ; and the change in him for the better the Lord has effected far away from you altogether. And so he is now not simply your bondman, but the Lord's freedman.

Suggestions. He will therefore be to you no longer as a slave only—whatever be the form and name of his social status—but doubly a brother. He is so to me, both in a natural and a spiritual sense; how much more to you must he stand in such relations? You will own in him, therefore, the fraternal bond of a common humanity ; and as a brother in Christ, you will yield to him the full right to partake in the privileges, it may be also the offices, of the Christian Church.

Yes; he and you and I are all on the level of brotherhood within the charmed circle of the Christian fellowship. Take him then to yourself as you would take me, if you would not risk breaking the sacred tie.

Not that I am vindicating his behaviour for a moment. Our Christian fellowship may forgive and overlook much in the spirit of that charity which covers a multitude of sins, but it can never relax the bonds of moral obligation nor connive at violations of right and duty. Equity demands that your just claims be honourably met.

If he have wronged you or caused you loss, that I may not seem to trifle with your private affairs, permit me to become his surety for the amount. I will refund you the whole. Witness my signature—Paul—in my own handwriting. Accept this pledge from me, that I may not have your reckoning up

70

A Familiar Paraphrase

how much more than this you stand in my debt,
owing me, as you do, no less than *your own self,*
besides what you now owe me for *him.*

Yes, brother, you *will* render me in the Lord a Expecta-
recompense of service, and let me enjoy some good, tions.
like yourself, from all this. I know you will. Do
refresh and cheer my heart in Christ! Not that
I have any misgivings as to the result, though I
thus warmly address you. I have full confidence,
while I write, in your willingness to comply with
the Divine requirements, and I know that you will
do more than I have permitted myself to say. And
when I mention my hope to visit you soon, you
can judge how thoroughly I am relying on you not
to disappoint my earnest desires.

Let me then further ask of you at this time to
provide me some lodging-place, for I am hopeful of
being by Divine mercy restored to you through your
united prayers on my behalf.

Epaphras, my fellow-captive in Christ Jesus, Farewells.
saluteth thee. So likewise do my fellow-labourers
now with me, Mark, Aristarchus, Demas, and Luke.
The grace of the Lord Jesus Christ be with the
spirit of you all to sanctify and bless. (Amen.)

71

EXPOSITION

ADDRESS AND SALUTATION

I

NAME AND TITLE OF THE WRITER

PHILEMON verse 1

PAUL, a prisoner of Jesus Christ.

Philemon 1. THIS is the only Epistle Paul begins by simply designating himself 'a prisoner.' Usually it is Paul 'an apostle,' or 'a servant of Jesus Christ.' He here omits the official title, because he writes as a friend asking a favour not as enforcing it with an air of authority.

'A prisoner,' why emphasised.

We should observe that Paul makes no fewer than *six* different allusions in this letter to the fact of his being now a prisoner or bondsman for Christ. Thus in verse 1 : 'Paul, a *prisoner* of Jesus Christ'; verse 9 : 'Paul the aged, and now also a *prisoner* of Jesus Christ'; verse 10: 'Onesimus, whom I have begotten in *my bonds*'; verse 13: 'That he might have ministered unto me in the *bonds* of the gospel'; verse 22: 'I trust that through your prayers I *shall be given unto you*'; and verse 23: 'Epaphras my *fellow-prisoner*.' Not that he dwells on this in any spirit of display or boasting on his own account;

72

he was incapable of the weakness. No one will **Philemon**
find the least trace of egotism or any taint of self- **I.**
seeking in such references.

Paul's purpose is purely a benign one. He
desires to touch a chord of tenderness in Philemon's
heart, and make it thrill with the subtle influences
of a relenting mood towards Onesimus. He means
to render it difficult for Philemon to say 'No' to
an appeal from a suffering confessor of Christ.

For Paul lays stress not on his imprisonment so **Cause of his**
much as on its cause. A prisoner *for Christ Jesus.* **Imprison-**
ment.
He was a voluntary sufferer, from no whimsical
caprice (as if he chose hardship for its own sake),
and still less from any fault or crime of his own, but
solely from conscientious steadfastness and devoted
attachment to Christ. This alone accounted for his
bonds.

Not that we are to think of the apostle as *at* **Nature of**
this time immured in a dungeon-cell. It was his **his Imprison-**
ment.
first imprisonment, when he was permitted to dwell
in a hired lodging of his own, and allowed, by the
kindness of the Prætorian Prefect named Burrhus
(to whose care he was committed, the one of Nero's
chief officers who was the most humane and up-
right), to be somewhat at large, while awaiting
trial before the Emperor.

It was, however, a weary and anxious two years,
and must now have been painfully irksome. Paul's
case was kept hanging so long in cruel suspense;
probably, as has been supposed, from the loss of the
documents connected with his 'appeal' in the shipwreck at Malta, or from the reluctance of the

The Epistle of St Paul to Philemon

Philemon
I. accusers to come forward early, or from the law's own delay, and caprice of the Cæsar.

During all the days and nights of this protracted captivity, the apostle was subjected to grievances and hardships which, while lighter than what most prisoners were familiar with in those times, greatly surpass our modern notions of even rigorous confinement.

His 'hired house' and 'chain.' The 'hired house' of which we read (Acts xxviii. 30) was 'by no means the comfortable residence one might suppose it to have been. The stately marble palace of the Emperor, like the other patrician mansions of Rome, was surrounded by wooden huts and cabins tenanted by the innumerable train of slaves, minions, and freedmen, who were retained for the service of the palace and its inmates. And it was in one of these miserable dens that the apostle was permitted to reside, instead of being cast into the vast horrible dungeons beneath the palace floor. Night and day, moreover, he was chained to soldier after soldier of the imperial guard, no moment of privacy allowed him, and was often treated with insolence, if not with violence, by the rude mercenaries.'

Samuel Cox, *Private Letters of St Paul and St John.* Some have thought that Paul's humble lodging—'his hired house'—was out in the general city, perhaps in the low and densely-peopled Jewish quarter (corresponding to the modern Ghetto); but in all probability, so long as he was in military keeping, the accommodation he paid for would require to be convenient for the soldiers and immediately under official supervision. There is no reason to suppose he was ever removed, during his *first* confinement, from the 'Prætorium,' where it is known

74

he was originally placed (Philipp. i. 12, 13). The **Philemon** Great Prætorium proper was a huge camp just **I.** outside the walls of the city; but as its soldiers furnished the body-guard of the Emperor, and the sentinels of the palace, they had a Prætorium, or See barrack, just behind the imperial buildings. In his and *second* imprisonment (between the two occurred the Howson's great fire of Rome, for which the Christians suffered *St Paul*, so severely) the apostle was probably thrust aw: vol. ii. p. 448. in the horrible Mamertine dungeon, or Tullianum, beneath the Capitol itself.

We dwell on the circumstances of his imprisonment —we fondly recall his vexatious position—because the whole 'surroundings' of this letter lend additional effect to its inherent grace. It is when the fragrant herb is *pressed* that it gives forth the richest odour; and it is when Paul's heart is being tried that it breathes out the tenderest sympathy.

Himself a bondman, 'with gyves upon his wrist,' Wronged, he pleads the cause of that other bondman, whose but not story is the burden of the letter. It is when himself embittered. a much-wronged captive that he begs forgiveness for a wrong-doer, and when society is making war upon himself he plays the part of peace-maker with others.

As dewdrops are seen to best advantage on the blades of grass from which they hang, or as gems sparkle brightest in their own appropriate settings, so we may reckon the apostles' imprisoned condition to be the fittest one for so rich a display of Christian spirit at its highest and noblest.

With what a sweet sense of inward peace and

The Epistle of St Paul to Philemon

freedom the prisoner goes forth on the spirit of his mission of blessing and goodwill:

> 'Stone walls do not a prison make,
>   Nor iron bars a cage ;
> Minds innocent and quiet take
>   That for a hermitage.
> If I have freedom in my love,
>   And in my soul am free,
> Angels alone that soar above
>   Enjoy such liberty.'[1]

Wrongs and oppressive suffering may drive even wise men mad ; but here it only seems to evoke Paul's tenderest feelings, and open wide the sluices of his affectionate sympathies.   Yes! *his* is :

> 'A heart at leisure from himself
>   To soothe and sympathise.'

How freely and naturally there drop from his pen the genial salutations of *Brother,* of *Brother beloved,* and the like ; or such words as '*grace*' and '*peace,*' '*love*' and '*joy*' that stud the page, and that are, each one of them, the keynote of holy sentiments of goodwill that animate his soul.   There is even something of pleasantry and humour in some pleadings of the letter, to render them more effectual and likely of success.

The cheerful, the tender, the kindly spirit is mingled throughout with a principle of inflexible loyalty to Christ.   For, feeling it an honour to suffer for Christ, he can afford to quietly wing his **way**

---

[1] Richard Lovelace's poem *To Althaea from prison,* 1642.

76

Name and Title of the Author

above all the gusts of resentful and malignant
passion, and far from the gloom of peevish sullenness
and embittered severity.

Has any other name stimulated like that of Christ
a spirit of such an unyielding and vehement attachment, combined with so benignant and gracious a
temper? There have been names and causes that
have sufficed to create a very whirlwind of excitement
in their favour, and have succeeded in arousing
mighty feelings that have swept like a tornado
through the bosoms of millions, but alas! like the
tornado, they have, as they surged along, carried
desolation and horror in their train.

History presents us, for example, with such a
phenomenon as the rise and spread of Moham-
medanism, whose adherents displayed an ardour of
attachment to their prophet which no disaster could
extinguish, and which death itself could not appal;
but what fierce and truculent passions sullied their
high devotedness! Violence and hostility were the
breath of their nostrils, and their watchword was
simply, 'Submit to the prophet, or the sword.' Or
we witness the spectacle of corrupt Christianity
arousing in its own support a marvellous glow of
adhesion from its votaries; but with what a cruel
eye it glared upon its victims, and with what dire
anathemas and inquisition-machinery it carried
persecution and slaughter wherever it could set down
its foot!

Oh! how easy to create for names and systems a
burning zeal that shall blaze out with scorching and
destructive flame!

The Epistle of St Paul to Philemon

Philemon I.

Inflexibly faithful, yet tender and forgiving.

Oh! how vastly different the genuine Christian spirit here displayed!

Paul, with a glow of loyal faithfulness to Christ, will never lapse into 'Saul the *persecutor*' again. If in him there is an ardour of attachment to Christ which it may please some to call bigotry and fanaticism, because it led him to prison, and which may seem Quixotic in its tenacity to those whose natures are incapable of similar self-abandonment and consecration to a holy cause, yet let it be confessed that the sublimest attachment to Christ is here found gloriously associated with all that is humane and gentle, and benign and tender.

II

FRIENDLY GREETINGS AND COMPLIMENTS

PHILEMON verses 1, 2

PAUL, a prisoner of Jesus Christ, and Timothy the brother,
To Philemon the beloved, and our fellow-labourer, and to Apphia the sister, and to Archippus our fellow-soldier.

Philemon I, 2.

Greetings to Philemon and family.

THE tact displayed by the apostle in keeping within the limits of Philemon's family and religious circle, when writing on a purely domestic matter, has been much and deservedly admired. He addresses the letter directly to Philemon, the head of the house; but he embraces in its opening salutations such others as had a special right to be informed of the case.

In associating Timothy with himself, he would evidently intimate that they were both heartily at one in the view they took of the matter in the letter,

78

a circumstance that would weigh with Philemon, **Philemon**
especially if we accept the conjecture that Timothy, **I, 2.**
who is emphatically called 'the brother,' was, like
the apostle himself, a personal friend of Philemon,
from whose very neighbourhood indeed he came. A
suit thus preferred and seconded could hardly fail to
command respectful attention and favour at the
outset.

It is also pretty generally understood that the
'beloved Apphia' (or rather, *sister* Apphia, as the
correct reading runs) is the wife of Philemon, the
connection of the names putting the matter beyond
reasonable question.

What a tribute of respect the gospel was beginning **Christian**
to teach men to pay to woman, and to attach to the **respect for Women.**
female head of the house as co-partner with the
husband ! What sacred names it makes of wife and
mother ! What mighty influences it recognises as
involved in them ! Here the apostle indicates how
Apphia had a right to be consulted, and the privilege
to be summoned to take a Christian and enlightened
interest in the matters that affect a Church or household's credit and well-being.

With considerable assurance we may further infer
that Archippus was the son and heir in the house, as
well as a chief office-bearer in the Church, either at
Colossæ or Laodicea (which was within easy walking
distance), he being an inmate of his father and
mother's dwelling.

He is here honoured by the distinguished designation from the apostle of 'our fellow-soldier,' while
at the close of the Epistle to the general Colossian

The Epistle of St Paul to Philemon

**Philemon
1, 2.**

**Genial
pleasantry.** Church the well-known charge is given about him that fits every young pastor: 'Say to Archippus, Take heed to the ministry which thou hast received in the Lord, that thou fulfil it.' The whole letter is rich in what Chrysostom calls 'spiritual pleasantries.' One of these is Paul's agreeable playing with proper names—a very characteristic habit of Jewish writing. Thus this last name Archippus is evidently an inversion of Hipparchus, a well-known *military* designation. The apostle seems to have this in his mind when he salutes Archippus as his fellow-*soldier*. So the name Apphia was originally a Phrygian nursery-word of endearment. Phrygian slave-women were to a large extent employed over the Roman Empire as nursery-maids, and they had widely familiarised their young charges with many juvenile Phrygian terms—Apphia being the one in special use between brothers and sisters. Hence the suitableness of '*sister*' Apphia. And no less fitly is Philemon addressed as 'the beloved,' that being really the meaning of the name; as the simple German lines interpret the idea of affection and friendly attachment it conveys :—

PHILEMON AN SEINEN FREUND.

Durch Dich ist die Welt mir schön,
Ohne Dich würd' ich sie hassen ;
Für Dich leb' ich ganz allein,
Um Dich will ich gern erblassen.
Gegen Dich soll kein Verläumdar
Ungestraft sich je vergehn ;
Wider Dich kein Feind sich waffnen,
Ich will Dir zur Seite stehn.

Friendly Greetings and Compliments

Which may be rendered thus :—

PHILEMON TO HIS FRIEND.

'Through thee the world is fair to me,
Without thee hateful would it be ;
For thee, for thee alone live I,
And for thee would I freely die.
No slanderer shall with his lie
Offend thee with impunity ;
Against thee rise no enemy,
But ever stand by thee will I.'

Special significance attaches to the three words which the apostle has here been applying to himself. The '*prisoner* for Christ Jesus' claims to be regarded as a '*labourer*' and a '*soldier*' by saluting Philemon and Archippus, the one as his *fellow*-labourer, the other his *fellow*-soldier.

Such coincidences of Scripture expression are worth noting ; for so great is the wealth of these sacred repositories that their treasure lies not only in golden masses, but overflows in rich veins of suggestiveness from even the most casual associations.

The preface begins with Paul in bonds, but leads up to Paul at prayer—the interval telling of work and warfare, culminating in worship as the ' Church in the house' rises to our view, with the devout benediction following.

We are permitted to look in on the 'prisoner,' ever busy at his work, writing, teaching, thinking, preaching, 'labouring much in the Lord.'

We look past the lounging mercenary at his wrist. Not he but Paul is fulfilling the true soldiership of

F 81

The Epistle of St Paul to Philemon

Philemon
I, 2.
The active
and the
devotional
in Religion.
the world. We see the apostle's work, by its intensity, rising into warfare; and as we hear him in his prayers the warfare rises into worship before the Lord.

What minglings of the active and the devout elements of religious life in the spirit of the apostle!

Virtues are often classed as *active* and *passive*— a distinction arising out of the condition of *doing* and the condition of *suffering* incident to the common human lot. Both of these phases of virtue Paul was now in a position to exemplify, subject as he was to the hardships of an irksome confinement, and yet not wholly restrained from opportunities of active labour for Christ.

How admirably he adjusts himself to each side of his circumstances! As 'an ensample of long-suffering and patience,' we have already noted in him a magnanimous superiority to bitterness or malice, to moodiness or murmuring.

His, however, is not only 'the patience of the saints'—his also is their 'patient continuance in *well-doing*.' When he calls Philemon his '*fellow-labourer*,' he is not to be understood as indicating resemblances in the outer forms of their work, but the inward reality of a common service for Christ. They are co-operators together *in Him*.

And what noble work the apostle is still permitted to do! He throws open his dwelling, like Philemon, for Christian uses—albeit *his* is only 'a hired house.' But if it were only a humble hut, it becomes a sanctuary. Prisoner though he is, he does not cease

Friendly Greetings and Compliments

to be the preacher. Many of his keepers he takes Philemon captive in the name of the Lord : and of the imperial I, 2. guards that have him in charge, what numbers he enlists as soldiers of the cross !

Paul indeed loves to think of himself as a *soldier ;* His strenuous Work. for in all earnest work there is verily something of war. Real labour itself is but a war against sloth and self-indulgent idleness. Agricultural labour is war on the weeds and the stubbornness of the soil. And so shall all work that kindles into the white heat of earnestness burst often into a war-flame.

'And to Archippus our fellow-soldier.' This is more than fellow-labourer. Its tone is more serious, for it has reference to the hardships and perils in the open field of the Church militant. Work *for* the world means war *in* it. For 'all virtues are fighting ones,' says St Bernard. And though 'the weapons of this warfare are not carnal,' neither materially carnal, as of steel or iron, nor (what needs more to be observed) morally carnal, as malice or envy, the summons to arms is ever in clear, crisp, and emphatic terms : 'Fight the good fight of faith ;' 'Strive for the mastery :' 'Put on the whole armour of God ; 'War a good warfare.'

Christian work is a soldierly campaign—a martial His Warring and Watching. service under authority, with a sacred meaning and incentive in it, and a grandly comprehensive issue before it, to raise it above drudgery or cheerless toil.

It includes the watching of the sentinel no less than the warring of the combatant—a watching that turns in every direction, looking *in* on the citadel of

83

The Epistle of St Paul to Philemon

the heart, looking *out* for the foe at hand, looking *around* for fellow-soldiers and associates, and above all, looking *up* for direction, help and blessing—'watching unto prayer.'

None of these does the apostle intermit, and least of all does he forget the exercises of devotion to hallow and enrich the fellowships and activities of life—'always in my prayers.'

The seat of these sacred reunions in work and war, in watching and wrestling, we are now to recognise as the apostle goes on to salute the *Church* in the house, with desires for grace and peace.

III

SALUTATION TO THE CHURCH-FELLOWSHIP

PHILEMON verse 2

AND to the Church in thy house.

THIS is an exceedingly happy and memorable phrase, 'the Church in thy house.' It links so interestingly and suggestively the Church and the family—the Church a 'whole *family* in heaven and earth,' and the family an emblem and dim reflection of 'the house of God which is the Church of the living God.'

Our noblest instincts gather round these two Divine institutions. The 'wise,' says our great modern poet, are those who, like the skylark,

'Soar, but never roam ;
True to the *kindred* points of *Heaven* and *Home*.'

But what we have specially to observe at present

84

is that the apostle, writing simply as a private Christian, manifests the liveliest interest in this Church, *as a Church*, no less than in individual members of it.

How his heart warms to the little company of disciples permitted to gather for Christian fellowship under the roof of the pious Philemon! All the best interpreters are agreed that Paul here salutes not the family and dependents of Philemon, but the organised Christian society accommodated with a meeting-place in his house. This seems evident from the use of the phrase in the parallel cases, Rom. xvi. 5 ; 1 Cor. xvi. 19 ; and Coloss. iv. 15.

The word rendered 'Church' refers always in the New Testament (where it occurs 115 times) to a fellowship of persons, never to a place of worship —this latter usage springing up naturally when separate buildings began to be erected for Christian assemblies early in the third century. A building, however, is but the seat and scene of what can never be wholly localized.

The word 'house' is properly either a 'home,' or an 'apartment' in a dwelling. It is the name throughout the Acts of the Apostles for the worship-rooms, or meeting-places, of the primitive Christian associations, as in Acts ii. 46, 'Breaking bread from meeting-place to meeting-place,' not from one private dwelling to another. So in Acts v. 42 ; and again viii. 3, 'Saul made havoc of the Church (association), entering into every *worship-apartment*, and haling men and women committed them to prison.' But what a change had been effected by his conversion!

The Epistle of St Paul to Philemon

Philemon 2. How different his whole spirit and attitude towards what he had striven to destroy.

Church and Home. Devoted attachment to the Church of Christ in all its far-scattered societies had long signalised the Apostle and been a powerful principle in his life. Years before this, when he had just become a Christian convert, we read that 'he assayed to join himself to the disciples' (Acts ix. 26). Nor did the ardour of his attachment become less intense, but seemed to glow with ever-increasing warmth, till in his 'care for all the Churches daily,' it might be said of him, as the Lord had said of Himself: 'The zeal of Thine house hath eaten Me up."

In thus remembering '*the* Church,' the association of disciples—whether in 'the house,' or wherever outwardly domiciled, matters not:

'God attributes to *place* no sanctity,
If none be thither brought by men,
Who there frequent or therein dwell :'

A Christian Churchman. Paul shows us what it is to be a true Churchman, such as every Christian should covet to be. For 'where Christ is, there is the Church.' And to be in Christ and have Christ in us is to be a Churchman indeed. This is not to be a mere local, national, or sectional Churchman, not an exclusively Ephesian, Colossian, Roman, Gallican, or Anglican, but, like Paul himself, a thoroughly *Christian* Churchman, and therefore, like him, a Churchman truly catholic, with a public-spirited regard for every Christian fellowship and for every Christian interest, in proportion as it *is* Christian.

Salutation to the Church Fellowship

From Christ alone, from Christ direct, had come **Philemon** with gracious and converting power to him the word **2.** of salvation.   Between himself and Christ had been transacted the sublime matter of his soul's peace on a sphere of conscience where none else may, without profanation, intrude.   The House of the Lord must never be put in the place of the Lord of the House. The Church's business is to proclaim the truth, to point the way and proffer the life, but it is the Lord's prerogative alone to say, I *am* the way, I *am* the truth, I *am* the life.

The Church, in the person of its messenger Ananias, **Place for the** could only 'show him what he must do;' by no **Church.** ordinances, however precious in themselves, availing to cure the sin-stricken soul, but only putting in his hand the healing prescription of the Great Physician, who alone can make him whole.

Taught thus in his own experience to derive everything from Christ and to depend on Him for all, he is yet not indifferent to the ordinance and fellowship of 'the Church.'

First and chiefly, as he is a prisoner of Christ, shut up entirely into Him for spiritual 'life and breath and all things,' he does not undervalue 'the Church.'   Needing not that any man teach him, and nursing his personal religion with the private exercises of devotion (*always in my prayers*, as he says, ver. 4), this does not make him independent of Church fellowship.

'It is not good for man to be alone.'   Christian **Need for the** life, though secret in its springs, and strictly personal **Church.** in its obligations, is not isolating in its temper.   Its

87

The Epistle of St Paul to Philemon

keenest instincts, its loveliest graces, are social in their operation.

> 'For solitude, however some may rave,
> Seeming a sanctuary, proves a grave:
> A sepulchre, in which the living lie,
> Where all good qualities grow sick and die.'

Embers which would speedily blacken and grow cold in separation, contribute by their mutual contact 'to make a solid core of heat.' Christ's people, by the very antagonism of worldly elements and associations around them, are drawn together for mutual support and countenance.

That tree must needs be a very hardy one that would successfully, by itself, defy the storms and rigour of an uncongenial clime. Under such untoward conditions trees grow best in groups—the one sustains and protects the other. 'Those that be planted (together) in the house of the Lord shall flourish in the courts of our God: they shall still bring forth fruit in old age' (Ps. xcii. 13, 14).

Guard against two Extremes. To neglect or despise the provisions and appointments of the House of the Lord, comes perilously near doing despite to the Lord of the House. We must ever guard against two opposite extremes: one the error of belated superstition where the Church is apt to be everything, the other the error of religious indifference which undervalues and passes it for nothing. But while the Church is in no sense the well-spring of life, as the ecclesiastical votary is apt to suppose, it is the region where the well-spring flows as the graceless despiser is apt to forget.

88

Salutation to the Church Fellowship

It is the whole of Christ's Church that the Apostle **Philemon 2.** here salutes in one of its branches ; regarding it as an appointed place where the disciples may 'gather themselves unto Jesus,' and where the LORD renews to them His gracious invitation, 'Come ye yourselves apart *with Me* into a solitary place, and rest awhile.'

> 'Such solitude sometimes is best society,
> And short retirement urges sweet return.'

The bee cannot gather honey on the wing. It must settle on the flower for a little if it would suck in the nectar. No more can Christ's disciples gain refreshment and sustenance in the midst of the world's bustle, save by habitually alighting and drawing on the resources of Christ's presence and grace afforded in the assemblies of the saints.

Not as though the 'Church' were only a con- **How to use the Church.** valescent home for recruiting spiritual energies—it is no less a field for their exercise and development. It is the seat and centre of *witnessing* for Christ and of *working* for Him. His disciples need not think to carry dark lanterns. Loyalty to Him will not be ashamed to confess His name before men. Like Christ Himself, it 'cannot be hid'—at least, not long—without dishonour to Him and disaster to itself.

> 'All is not gold that shines, 'tis true.
> But all that is gold ought to shine.'

Paul therefore hails the Church as the fit rallying-ground for all who would most effectively own Christ and engage in His service. It is the institution through which to exert the full influence of Christian

The Epistle of St Paul to Philemon

life and zeal. For Christian energy and Christian labour will be, in measure, Church energy and Church labour too.

The apostle, for example, hopes to do something for his convert Onesimus, through the Church he here salutes. He seeks to lodge him in his bosom, and secure for him a share in all the blessings of its fellowship.

Church's
Mission and
Work.

For as the lowly bush receives the dew of heaven, not to absorb it on itself, but to distil a portion on the yet lowlier plant that may grow at its root, so must 'the Church in the house' learn 'to do good and distribute,' as a steward for Christ of that gospel which is committed to it, in trust for others. Even the lordly mountain catches the first outpourings of the skies, not to treasure them up in its own bosom, but to send them down in limpid and refreshing streams along the valleys and meadows below.

And so it is the mission of the Church of Christ at large to fulfil such offices of gospel mercy as shall make 'the wilderness and solitary place be glad for them, and the desert rejoice and blossom as the rose,' and to be the instrument of Christian enterprise and effort to the ends of the earth.

On these and similar accounts, Paul never forgets to display a public-spirited interest in 'the Church,' and loses no opportunity of recognising its claims and identifying himself with its fellowships.

> 'For her my tears shall fall ;
> For her my prayers ascend ;
> To her my cares and toils be given
> Till cares and toils shall end.'

The General Benediction

THE GENERAL BENEDICTION

PHILEMON verses 3-7

GRACE to you, and peace, from God our Father, and the Lord Jesus Christ.

THIS benediction is the ordinary one used by Paul **Philemon** at the opening of his Epistles, except that in his **3-7.** three Pastoral Letters 'mercy' is introduced between 'grace' and 'peace.' It is worthy of notice that grace and peace are a combination of classical and Jewish modes of salutation—the Oriental amid habitual disturbance saying 'peace' to the friend he meets, and the Western peoples under more settled government using a word which, as savouring somewhat of heathenism, the apostle, by a slight alteration, transforms into its nearest Christian likeness, 'grace'—a fact how significant of the all-embracing and unifying faith of the gospel, covering East and West alike with its outstretched hands of blessing! It is not a mere kindly greeting of common courtesy, but a religious invocation.

There are two kindred forms of pious expression, **Doxology** with which we are rendered familiar from their **and Benediction.** frequent recurrence in Scripture and the place they hold in the exercises of worship. These are the *Doxology* and the *Benediction*, which stand alone as hallowed modes of blessing.

The spirit of both is intensely devotional—the doxology being the consummation or crowning

The Epistle of St Paul to Philemon

**Philemon
3-7.** utterance of *praise to God*, the benediction, of *prayer for man*. The one aims at blessing God by ascription, the other at blessing man by petition or supplication. In neither case is blessing actually or directly conferred; the doxology attributing blessedness to God, the benediction beseeching for blessedness to man.

**Nature of a
Benediction.** There is something of doxology thus in every apostolic benediction. For we cannot too deeply realise that the apostles never arrogate to themselves any prerogative to bestow such blessings as grace and peace. The benediction is not in itself a benefaction. To utter it is not to *grant*, but to *crave* from God the desired boon. It is a prayer, dependent for its efficacy on the Divine promises, and on the believing and benevolent desires of him who offers it. 'Grace to you and peace' come neither from nor through the apostles as channels, but 'from God the Father and the Lord Jesus Christ.'

**Contents of
this Benedic-
tion.** Paul therefore, here as elsewhere, when casting a loving glance towards friends on earth, accompanies it with an earnest up-look towards 'Him that dwelleth in the heavens.' His ardent and most cordial well-wishes are couched in the language of fervid supplication. And this prayer is a summary of all the blessings the Divine hand can bestow or the human heart possess. For 'grace' is the exhaustless spring of all mercies in God, and 'peace' is the blessed draught of grace that slakes our immortal thirst.

We may conceive of 'grace and peace' being

The General Benediction

connected with 'God our Father and the Lord Jesus Philemon
Christ,' as we conceive of the water with which a 3-7.
town is supplied in relation to the reservoir of storage
on the one hand, and the channel of communication
and distribution on the other.

We may think of God our Father as the exhaust- Relations of
less fount of these perennial blessings—He is 'the Grace and Peace.
God of all grace,' and the 'very God of peace.' Yet
all this grace and peace are not gathered up in Him
like water in some lake from which there is no
outlet, but, like reservoir supplies, these unspeakable
mercies are meant to be communicated and enjoyed
through the channel and conduit of the Lord Jesus
Christ.

And while the whole appliances are regulated
and managed by the continual operation of the Holy
Ghost, there is nothing derogatory to that Divine
Spirit, although in this salutation no specific mention
is made, in so many words, of His work and offices,
because the greater function includes all the separate
distributions for individual use and benefit.

Grace therefore is peace prepared for us, and peace
is grace enjoyed by us. For grace is simply that
free favour that spontaneously emanates from love—
the grace of God our Father and the Lord Jesus
Christ being the self-moved and self-moving operations of Divine love to sinful men. Such kindness
is called 'grace' because the inherent goodness of the
Divine disposition alone can account for it ; 'grace'
being the word that brings into special prominence
the Divine motive in redemption as unbought, un-
sought, and unconstrained by principles from without,

The Epistle of St Paul to Philemon

just as 'mercy' has reference particularly to the unworthy character of its objects.

Grace a many-sided Word.

A many-sided word like grace is best explained by analogies suggested by some similar many-sided word, such as *life, vegetation,* and the like.

Grace, like life, may be regarded as a great and blessed gift from without, or a Divine power working mercifully towards us, and ultimately working in us; bringing salvation for us, and securing its mightiest triumph when it secures a lodgment of itself within us. And just as life receives various names from the various blessings it includes—feeling, moving, seeing, hearing, which are but varieties of the one great privilege of living—so grace is the comprehensive term including the supply of all favours and privileges needful for our fallen and undeserving condition as sinners to be saved. It is enlightenment for darkness; pardon for transgression; comfort for trial; hope for despondency; strength for weakness, and all help for all need.

And just as life brought into play as a power within us will be sight, if it operate through the eye: speech, if through the tongue: hearing, if through the ear; so with grace—if it work upon our convictions of sin, it will be the grace of repentance: if on God's testimony, it is the grace of faith: if on God's commandments, it is the grace of obedience—and so on through the whole range of Christian excellence.

Grace in its various applications.

We thus use 'grace' with the varied applications attachable to any kindred word, like 'vegetation;' as when we say, 'Vegetation is at work,' we mean

The General Benediction

Philemon 3-7. the hidden power or influence which produces the buds, leaves, fruits, and all the riches and beauty of the face of nature ; or when, on the other hand, we say, 'Vegetation is looking lovely,' we refer to the effects themselves of the hidden power as they strike and delight the eye.

So grace is the Divine agency or quickening power which, when it takes hold of us, produces all good thoughts, all holy desires, and all heavenly life, while it is no less the name for those thoughts, desires, and graces themselves, considered as its fruits.

If further it be viewed as dealing with Divine truth and promise, with God's gospel-message of mercy, with Christ and His work, with the Holy Spirit's aid, with the heavenly inheritance, and the like, under the aspect of blessings appropriated and enjoyed, then *grace* becomes *peace*. When, in short, we think of spiritual and saving benefits as connected with the Divine nature, and as communicated through our Lord Jesus Christ, we call them all *grace* ; and, on the other hand, we call them all *peace* when we think of them with special relation to our own good, when we think of their precious value for us, and their tranquillising and enjoyable effects upon us.

Oh! if our peace were not of grace, we should Our Peace all of Grace. be doon.ed to perish for want of it, like a population whose whole water supply depended on two or three trickling streams that might dry up and fail when most needed. If we are to live beyond the fear of our peace getting exhausted, it must be by drawing on the perennial resources of heavenly grace, ever full and ever flowing among the everlasting hills—

The Epistle of St Paul to Philemon

Philemon 3-7.
A fervent Appeal. the free, the sovereign, the regal, the self-moving and redeeming love of God in Christ Jesus our Lord.

What an appeal there is to Philemon in such a benediction! As if the apostle would say, 'This is sufficient to enable you to do all I am to ask at your hands. And as you would find grace and favour with the Lord yourself, or enjoy peace in your own soul, you may not be inexorable or ungracious towards Onesimus, but must seek peace and pursue it, by sealing its comforts on the penitent's heart.'

THE EXORDIUM OR PROLOGUE

PHILEMON verses 4-7.

I THANK my God always, making mention of thee in my prayers, hearing of thy love and faith, which thou hast toward the Lord Jesus, and unto all the saints; that the fellowship of thy faith may become effectual, in the knowledge of everything good that is in us, unto Christ Jesus. For I had much joy and consolation in thy love, because the hearts of the saints have been refreshed by thee, brother.

PRELIMINARY NOTE

THIS prologue or exordium is somewhat intricate and involved. The difficulties of the passage dis-appear, however, when we construe verses 4-7 as *one long sentence*, and observe that it is a remarkable illustration of the grammatical figure called *chiasm* (or crossing like letter X), whereby the different clauses are introverted, or put cross-wise, thus—

Philemon 4-7. This the difficult Passage.

The blind and dumb

both spake and saw. (The blind saw; the dumb spake.)

The principle is, to connect the first member of the sentence with the last, the second with the last but one, and so on—thus:

Give not that which is holy to the dogs,
Neither cast ye your pearls before swine,
Lest they trample them under feet,
And turn again and rend you;

G   97

The Epistle of St Paul to Philemon

where we see that it is the *swine* that are said to trample, and the *dogs* to turn again and rend.

Proceeding on this principle with the eight clauses of the present paragraph, we double the second four back upon the first four, each to each, so that one and eight shall be found to correspond, two and seven, three and six, and four and five—thus :—

I thank my God always,
  Making mention of thee in my prayers,
    Hearing of thy love,
      And faith, which thou hast
      Toward the Lord Jesus, and
    Unto all the saints.
  That the fellowship of thy faith may become effectual,
    etc.
For I had much joy and consolation in thy love.

Beginning at the central pair and proceeding outwards, we are thus led to see that what the apostle means to say is, that Philemon's faith is towards the Lord Jesus, and his love is to all the saints; that his prayers are specially about Philemon's faith, while his thankfulness is specially evoked by his joy at Philemon's love. The passage then reads thus: ' I thank my God (for I had much joy and comfort in thy love), making mention of thee in my prayers (*e.g.*, that the fellowship of thy faith may become effectual, in the knowledge of all good), hearing as I do of the faith thou hast (towards the Lord Jesus) and of thy love (for all the saints).'

Devout Thanks and Prayer

I

DEVOUT THANKS AND PRAYER.

I THANK my God always, making mention of thee in my prayers.
—Verse 4.

IN the very principle of gratitude imbedded in our Philemon nature may be found a powerful witness to the 4-7. personality of God. 'I thank my God,' says the Gratitude apostle : reminding us that thanks can be rendered demands a Personal to a person only. God.

Gratitude cannot be displayed towards an abstraction, or a blind force, or a dumb law, or any unresponsive object.

Every such exercise demands not some *thing*, but some *one* on whom it may go forth. Like other original sentiments of the heart, it 'cries aloud for the living God.' How fatuous therefore the notion J. S. Mill's broached by a distinguished philosopher. 'We *Comte and Positivism*, venture to think that a religion may exist without p. 133. belief in a God.' This certainly is not possible, if religion is to include worship. For thankful acknowledgments must be an element in religious worship.

Suppose a man has made a narrow escape in some disaster, because a certain wheel and axle did not break. He is devoutly thankful, but it cannot be *to* the wheel and axle. He may be thankful *for* this or *for* that contingency, but the question recurs, *To* what or *to* whom is he thankful? He must either cease cultivating this high and essential principle of his nature as a *religious* habit, and therefore *cease being religious*, or find the fitting object for it.

99

The Epistle of St Paul to Philemon

Philemon
4-7.
Religion
doubly
personal.

Religion is doubly a personal thing. Only a person can say 'I thank,' and only *of* or *to* a person can it be said. The only counterpart of a religious 'I thank,' is 'God,' '*my* God.'

Positivism itself cannot, as a *worship*, get rid of *a* God. It has to imagine a deity. It is forced to personify 'collective humanity,' and address *that* under a personal name of the 'Grand Etre,' a mock person instead of a real personal Being!

This living God Paul speaks of as '*My* God,' expressive at once of his personal interest in God and his entire surrender to God. It means both that God is mine and I am His.

Real
Religion
kills selfish-
ness.

How this refutes the charge sometimes preferred against religion, that it is in open league with the selfish motives and aims of the human heart! For he who thus unreservedly yields himself to another cannot be self-centred. To own God's claims is to break for ever with the spirit of self-seeking.

What evidence of this we have here! Vital godliness is intensely personal, yet it is intensely magnanimous and disinterested. For while Paul says, '*My* God,' he bursts forth, on the one hand, into praise and thanks to God, and, on the other, into earnest entreaty for Philemon.

Real religion—if by this we understand not mere groping and struggling after God, but having got conscious hold of Him and made a full surrender to Him—is ever nobly expansive. No self-seeking disposition can attain to its enjoyable experience. For dearly as human nature loves monopolies, it speedily finds there are objects which elude all

100

Devout Thanks and Prayer

attempts at monopolising, and mock at every Philemon 4-7. endeavour to subject them to selfish limitations.

God cannot be possessed except as a personal good, and yet cannot be possessed and enjoyed as a personal good *only*, any more than sunshine can be held as mere private property. The more of such blessings a neighbour enjoys, there is the more for any one else to use and enjoy. So there is that in vital personal interest in God which at once guarantees a thankful spirit in the possessor, and acts as a safeguard against the spirit of self-worship.

God cannot be mono-polised.

The law of the solar system is that 'the more quickly a planet revolves round the sun, the more slowly it turns round its own axis'; and the very principle which regulates its own speed makes it discharge its dutiful functions towards neighbouring orbs, while yet keeping it balanced in its own safe and sure course and at the proper angle of inclination round the central one of all.

No wonder there exhales from Paul's heart the incense of pure thanks to God for all the evidences of Philemon's goodness and grace, as inwrought by saving mercy, and as working outwardly in acts of love and kindness unto others! Far from the expression of his self-interest, '*My* God' being self-confined, his very thanks are absorbed with the good in another.

The more a fire shoots its flame and heat towards heaven, the farther out from itself will it shoot its warmth. So the more vehemently the soul can possess itself of God and be possessed by Him, the more ardently will it be carried upward with its

Religion never self-confined.

101

The Epistle of St Paul to Philemon

Philemon
4-7. thanks and outward with its intense desires for the good of others.

No wonder, therefore, that Paul, having thanked God as his own God, because of the faith in Christ Jesus and love to all saints He had graciously wrought into Philemon's heart, lets himself go forth in earnest prayer and desire that Philemon may obtain an enlarged fellowship with himself in every good thing which he enjoyed through Christ Jesus.

Thoughts of God's mercies will ever be found lying very close to thoughts of others' needs. To be able to thank God sincerely for the good we see in others is the best security for our feeling intensely solicitous for their further good. And perhaps nothing indicates more clearly the presence of an affectionate solicitude for others than prayer to God on their behalf, provided it be genuine prayer. For he who utters the deep desires of his heart in supplication to God will never be found dealing with his prayers as the ostrich with its eggs—no sooner dropped than covered over and forgotten—but as he who carefully sows seeds in the furrow, moving earnestly in the direction of his wishes and contributing in his own place as a fellow-worker with God toward their realisation.

Pray for others. One of the best things Paul desired for himself was to have 'a name and a place' in the prayers of others. This once secured, he was persuaded he should have no cause for complaining of any lack of interest or attention on their part. And as he is continually urging that 'prayer be made without ceasing by the Church unto God for him,' being

Devout Thanks and Prayer

unaware of any more effective means for securing common good, or evincing mutual interest, he delights in exemplifying in this highest form, the spirit of friendship, sympathy, and goodwill. Silver and gold he has none, but of the full wealth of his intercessions from the heart, how freely he gives!

The prayers of the apostle consist, in the present case, of *thanksgiving* and *intercession*—finding a starting-place from his own personal and conscious interest in God.

The same connection of ideas is often found in his other letters. Thus: ' I *thank my God* through Jesus Christ for you all. . . . Without ceasing I *make mention of you always in my prayers*' (Rom. i. 8); or, ' *I thank my God* upon every remembrance of you, always in *every prayer of mine for you all*' (Philipp. i. 3).

Some connect the word 'always' with the first clause: 'I always thank my God whenever I remember thee in my prayers'; others with the second: 'I thank my God, always (=habitually) remembering you in my prayers.'

The former view is probably correct; but it is of comparatively small moment how we place the word, provided we observe that Paul's prayer as an exercise of devotion or praise to God, precedes his prayer as an exercise of desire for man.

Prayer, like everything else in spiritual life, has two sides—an upper one, with its face towards God, and an under one, with its face toward man.

Do not many 'restrain prayer before God,' because they unduly magnify the human aspect of

103

The Epistle of St Paul to Philemon

devotion, and are chiefly concerned with the question, 'What *profit* is there if we pray to Him? Then, because they do not get all they wish, and find their prayers unattended by good, they grow lukewarm and barren in devotion—whereas they should, as the apostle here, and as Christ Himself in the 'Lord's Prayer,' give prominence and precedence to the Divine interests and the Divine praise, extolling God's name and rendering thanks before beginning to supplicate for ourselves or others. *First God's mercies, then human needs.*

II

REASONS FOR THE DEVOUT THANKS

HEARING of thy love and faith, which thou hast toward the Lord Jesus, and unto all the saints.—Verse 5.

Two Reasons. THIS verse assigns the reason why Paul thanks God at present. 'I thank my God . . . . hearing as I do of thy love for all saints, and the faith thou hast toward the Lord Jesus.'

Though the love is the fruit or result of the faith, it is here very fitly placed first. For though faith is first in the order of time and nature, yet love is here first in importance, because it is to Philemon's love that the apostle is to make his appeal.

Philemon's Faith and Love. Paul seizes on the two elements that constitute the sum and substance of all Christian life and character—the faith that worketh by love. For, as it is said, ' Fear God, and keep His commandments —this is the *whole man.*' So, ' Faith toward the

104

Reasons for the Devout Thanks

Lord Jesus and love to all saints,' this is the *whole* **Philemon**
Christian. **4-7.**

This faith embodies the theoretic principles of Christian life, while this love for saints embodies these principles on their practical side.

Like heart and lungs in the body, each has its own Relation of Faith to Love. functions ; and, though separate, the one never acts apart from the other—life being the combined play of both. Faith binds to all Christian verities, translating them into personal convictions ; while love binds to all Christian motives, translating these into personal activities—love being well called the daughter of faith and the mother of virtue and good works.

We should here note that the love is said to be *unto* the saints and the faith to be *toward* the Lord Jesus—a change of prepositions that is meant to indicate a delicate distinction between the physical nearness of saints, on whom may be poured forth the tokens of love in visible and tangible form, and the physical remoteness of the Lord Jesus, whom we cannot thus locally reach, but may simply direct our souls forward and upward *towards* Him, so long as we are on this lower sphere.

But HE must be the object of faith, if from its exercise this love to saints would inevitably flow— as inevitably as a stream from its fountain.

There is nothing simpler than faith. It is involved Faith is accepting Testimony. in every act of intelligence. And all faith is just the same thing, *considered as a process of the mind.* It is crediting something upon testimony—one act of faith differing from another mainly according to what or who it is that is credited.

The Epistle of St Paul to Philemon

The object that faith embraces is of as serious moment in Christian life as *what* the lungs breathe in natural life.   Faith towards the Lord Jesus is the believing what God testifies regarding Him.

No doubt we may believe many truths that God testifies regarding Him, and yet not have 'faith toward the Lord Jesus ' Himself, for we may believe a great deal that is true of a person, and not have faith toward the person himself.   But if there be not 'faith towards the Lord Jesus,' it arises simply from not exercising faith in some essential part or other of the full truth about Christ which God has testified.

The chief points in that testimony are these : That in our condition of sin and danger we individually need a Saviour ; that this Saviour is the Lord Jesus, the only begotten Son of God, whom God in His love for the world has sent forth to seek and save lost sinners of mankind ; that sinners must put their trust in Him, and must do this voluntarily, yet not without the help of Divine grace, so as to accept the free offer of pardon, peace, and purity at His hands ; and that every individual sinner is bound, authorised, warranted, and welcome to do so.

Some may have faith in these parts of the Divine testimony up to, perhaps, the last one of them, and yet not be 'shut up into the faith of Christ,' because their faith fastens *only* on historical facts, or theoretic ideas, or doctrinal truths about Christ, without going forward directly and completely to personally trusting Christ Himself, as they are commanded and bound to do.

Reasons for the Devout Thanks

Faith in the Lord Jesus is, no doubt, faith in His sacrifice; but it goes further in receiving the Divine testimony till it be faith also in ' *Him* sacrificed for us'; faith not only in the cross, but ' in *Him* crucified'; not faith in His righteousness only, but in ' Jesus Christ, the righteous,' the Lord our righteousness — in short, not only assent to truths regarding Christ, but trust toward and upon Himself.

Philemon 4-7. Faith in Christ means Trust in Him.

For faith is just like the coupling-chain of a railway-carriage — everything depends on where its fastenings are ultimately attached. The carriage moves only if its coupling-chain communicate with the moving power. And faith saves only as it takes hold of the Saviour for itself, and terminates in Him as its object.

This precious faith is a bond of attachment. It cannot be a single isolated act, but an abiding attitude of confidence towards the Lord Jesus. Not a mere contemplative attitude, however, for faith is not in an inert principle—it is a ceaselessly operative movement, vitally uniting to Christ and habitually appropriating all that is in Him. It can never be entirely of the past, therefore, but always of the present—not the faith thou *hadst*, but the faith thou *hast*; and necessarily making itself ' heard of ' sooner or later. ' *Hearing* of thy faith.'

This faith, in short, must *work*. When Hedley Vicars began to exercise it, for example, he bought a copy of the Scriptures and laid it on his barrack table, before he felt strong enough to break the intelligence otherwise to his ungodly comrades.

The Epistle of St Paul to Philemon

**Philemon
4-7.**

'As faithless works the Lord will not reward,
So workless faith the Lord will not regard.'

**Love is the
evidence of
Faith.**

But it must work *by love.* The word for love
here is a peculiarly Christian one. It is a pure New
Testament original, occurring nowhere in classical
Greek of the pre-Christian period. It is used
upwards of a hundred times in the New Testament,
while the fact that it occurs three times in verses
5-8, now before us, is one of those little, but significant, circumstances that serves to reveal the tone and
temper of this Epistle.

There is a Greek term for the passion of love, and
another for the kindly love that exists between
friends; but neither would suit the idea of a pure
and sacred affection conveyed by the word here
employed.

**Love
variously
expresses
Itself.**

This love is, of course, susceptible of various shades
of meaning, according to the object on which it is
exercised. Here it includes both *benevolent love,* that
is solicitous for the welfare of others; and *complacent
love,* that delights in the Christian and spiritual
excellences they may display—this latter idea being
emphasised by the word 'saints' in the present case.
It is for one of these 'saints' the apostle is about to
plead. And we will not think it strange, therefore,
that not love to the Lord Jesus Himself, but love to
His saints, is proposed here as the test of a living
faith—for it is the Lord Jesus who is loved in them.

The magnetised needle turns to the invisible North
Pole whenever it turns to *any* visible object that lies
due north of itself; and so, love to saints, as saints,

108

Purport of the Prayer for Philemon

is love to Christ Himself personally, because it is Philemon love to whatever of Christ is manifest in them. 4-7.

> 'In them HE may be cheered and fed,
> In them be warmed and clad.
> Ours be the blissful task to make
> Their downcast spirits glad.'

III

PURPORT OF THE PRAYER FOR PHILEMON

THAT the fellowship (arising out) of thy faith may become effectual, in the knowledge of everything that is good in us, unto Christ Jesus.—Verse 6.

PAUL having rendered *thanks*, proceeds now to the *prayer*.

Christian truth and experience are full of para- Paradoxes: doxes. 'Whosoever will lose his life for My sake,' their place
and use. says the Lord Himself, 'the same shall find it.' 'When I am weak,' says Paul, in another place, 'then I am strong.'

Such seeming contradictions are useful for arresting attention, and impressing some great principle on the mind. They fall on the ear with the insinuating influence of half-told secrets, that only whet curiosity the more.

We have a similar paradox here. No sooner has the apostle expressed himself thankful to God for blessings, than he begins with fresh applications. Devoutly thankful, as if satisfied with what God has done for Philemon, he yet goes on to plead for further largesses on his behalf.

The Epistle of St Paul to Philemon

Philemon
4-7.

Harmony of Thanks and Petition.

To the unspiritual and uninitiated mind this process looks mysterious, but it is the ordinary mystery of the Divine life in the soul.

Prayer is based on a supreme contentedness with Divine gifts and blessings, but also on a sublime uncontentedness with human attainments in them. It therefore catches up thankfulness and petition into a happy unity, as the railway-train holds its passengers at rest and yet in motion at the same moment. True prayer is free alike from querulous discontent and from cloddish self-content.

The very satisfaction of the traveller, at the well, with the water it affords, bids him draw more largely on its supply for himself and others. And so Paul is thankful for all that God is and does, for all He has and offers, as manifested in the evangelic faith and love of Philemon; but he cannot think of either Philemon or himself resting satisfied where so much more remains to be possessed.

To have nothing further to ask and yearn after were to have the mainspring of activity and improvement utterly broken. To pray is therefore a privilege and a relief. To pray for others is especially so to a loving and benevolent heart.

We might have been permitted to pray only for ourselves; but amid the separations and scatterings of earth God has been pleased to put intercession for one another as an instrument of mutual interest and blessing into the hands of all who would promote each other's good.

Paul had organised an extensive system of intercession throughout the Church at large, as all his Epistles

110

Purport of the Prayer for Philemon

attest—ever by his example commending the way to a throne of grace as the royal road for reaching and acting on distant loved ones, with the happiest results.

Philemon is far away in the region of Phrygia, but as Paul relies on being remembered by him and his friends ('I am hoping that through your prayers I shall be given unto you,' verse 22), he suits a prayer to his friend's special requirements, now that Philemon is brought prominently to his recollection. And this is to be regarded as an example of the apostle's customary private petitions at this time on Philemon's behalf: 'Making mention of thee in my prayers . . . that the fellowship of thy faith may become effectual, in the knowledge of everything good that is in us, unto Christ Jesus.'

This is unquestionably the most difficult verse in the Epistle. It is not easy to catch its exact meaning, the expressions are so condensed and abbreviated. This has cast a shade of obscurity over the precise sense of the prayer, and rendered it susceptible of different interpretations. There are, however, only two principal classes of translation (to which all minor varieties may be reduced) turning on the question: Is the word 'fellowship' to be taken in an active or a passive sense?

Taking it *actively*, it may mean either,

1. That the communication of thy faith (or the imparting of it) may become effectual in leading others to recognise all the good that is in us Christians (in US, not, *in you*, is the correct reading); or,

The Epistle of St Paul to Philemon

2. That the share which others get in thy faith (*i.e.*, in its fruits), or, in other words, that the beneficence and liberality of thy faith towards others may be effectual in leading them to recognise all the good that is in us.

There is a fatal objection, however, to the idea of ' fellowship ' being taken in this active sense here. It necessitates our understanding the prayer as not being one for Philemon himself, but one rather on behalf of others—he being prayed for simply as an instrument of good, while his own spiritual condition is subordinated to that of others.

We conceive, however, that the direct object of the apostle is to pray for Philemon's own personal advancement in the grace and knowledge of Christ, and of all that makes for the Master's honour.

Two possible renderings.
There is, moreover, a strong objection to No. 1, because the notion of a man imparting his faith, or inoculating others with its grace, is not in accordance with the apostle's usage in prayer ; and the present phrase is not at all parallel to the sense of our Lord's words : ' Let your light so shine before men, that they may see your good works, and glorify your Father which is in heaven.' While if No. 2 were correct, we should have expected Paul to have written, ' that the fellowship of thy love,' if mere beneficence or liberality were all the apostle intended.

We understand ' fellowship,' therefore, in its broader passive sense of communion ; and the following we take to be the meaning of the prayer ' That the fellowship (or communion) springing from

Purport of the Prayer for Philemon

the faith thou hast, may be effective in promoting
the honour of Christ, by your discerning and approving of everything that is Christianly good in us,
whether in the way of truth or duty, of privilege or
practice.'

The subject of prayer is Philemon's part or lot
in what the apostle calls 'the fellowship or communion'—the great commonwealth or co-partnership
in Christ whereby His people realise their spiritual
unity. 'Faith toward Christ' constitutes the bond
of this fellowship, serving as it does the twofold
purpose of *introducing* any one into co-partnership
with Christ, and of *producing* in any one the affinity
or spiritual kinship of character inseparable from it.

The apostle does not say '*thy* fellowship' (for the
fellowship is really Christ's), but as the faith must
be Philemon's, he puts it 'the fellowship of thy
faith,' or rather, to be more accurate, 'the fellowship
of the faith of thee'—not, therefore, 'the fellowship
or participation of others in thy faith and its acts, but
the fellowship of the faith which thou hast.'

Regarding this fellowship, so far as Philemon's
relation to it was concerned, the apostle proceeds to
pray that it might not be an inert or dormant thing,
but of some practical and tangible service—'that the
fellowship springing out of the faith which thou hast
may manifest its energy and efficiency in a full knowledge of all that is good amongst us to the praise and
honour of the Lord Jesus Christ, who is alike your
Lord and mine.'

It is particularly worthy of notice, that 'knowledge,' as the boundless field in which the Christian

The Epistle of St Paul to Philemon

Philemon
4-7.
See Coloss.
i. 9 ; Philipp.
i. 9, and
Ephes. i. 17.
fellowship should exercise itself, is a favourite word
with the apostle in the three prison Epistles contemporary with the present one, being introduced
into the opening prayer of them all. These parallel
passages determine that it is Philemon's own Christian
knowledge, not that of others, Paul has here in view.

This 'knowledge of all good,' in which the fellowship of 'faith toward the Lord Jesus' must learn to
expatiate, if it would perfect itself as a Christian
fellowship, is of course much more than a mere
speculative knowledge, and includes a wise and
intelligent apprehension of Christian truth and duty,
vital sympathy with the principles and aims of Christ,
and practical submission to His requirements. For
the goal of such efforts must be 'unto Christ Jesus;'
that is, to the intent of promoting His honour and
exalting the glory and credit of His name among
men.

There is a possible reference to the 'tree of
knowledge of good and evil,' with the hint that
the knowledge of Christ is a knowledge of all good,
and no evil. Goodness must, in short, never be
dissociated from the name of Christ, nor must any
evil of any kind be ever associated with it in any
degree.

Good Intentions require regulating. A painful proverb reminds us that 'mischief often
begins in the name of the Lord.' There may be a
sincere and well-meant desire to do many things
'unto Christ Jesus;' but the intention to do Him
honour may, alas! not be regulated by an adequate
'knowledge' of what it becomes any one to do, who
would rightly represent Christ and His cause.

114

Purport of the Prayer for Philemon

To guard against passing a counterfeit coin, there **Philemon** must be attention paid not merely to the image and **4-7·** superscription it professes to bear, but to the quality of the metal of which it is composed. A pure wish to do everything 'unto Christ' is the noblest of motives; but the wish, in order to be pure, must be informed by this 'knowledge' of everything good that relates to truth and duty.

These devout wishes of the apostle on behalf of Philemon are expressed in general terms, but we cannot mistake their special reference.

Paul has Onesimus in his mind; and this de- **Real Aim of** termines the current of the prayer. The Lord had **the Prayer.** wrought faith and love in the heart of the bondman. Here was one 'good thing.' Paul and Timothy had recognised and owned, on very sufficient and satisfactory evidence, the conversion of Onesimus, and had received him into their Christian fellowship. Here was another 'good thing'—at least they thought it right and dutiful.

Very different as yet were Philemon's ideas respecting Onesimus; and no wonder. But the apostle prays that Philemon's fellowship with Christ and with them might give a happy illustration of its effectiveness by readily recognising Christ wherever He is to be found; even in the hitherto Christless Onesimus.

If Paul and Timothy's views and feelings toward the bondman were Christianly 'good,' Philemon would adopt and act on them; and therefore Paul prays that they might all be *en rapport* in the matter; so that the fellowship might be preserved intact and

115

The Epistle of St Paul to Philemon

its unity realised, to the glory of Christ, and the
praise of His name.

> 'The honours of that name, 'tis just to guard ;
> They are a trust, but lent us, which we take,
> And should in reverence to the donor's fame,
> With care transmit them down to other hands.'

IV

GOOD OCCASION FOR THANKS

For I had much joy and consolation in thy love, because the
hearts of the saints have been refreshed by thee, brother.—Verse 7.

THIS verse stands connected not with the sentence
which immediately precedes, but with the opening
words of the passage : ' I thank my God always,
making mention of thee in my prayers.'

The apostle has already stated the ground of
reason of his thanksgiving and prayer. It was the
report he had heard of Philemon's faith and love.
He now assigns the cause or motive within himself
that prompted him to this outpouring of prayer with
thankfulness. It was the sense of joy and comfort
he felt at the delightful tidings : ' I thank my God
always, making mention of thee in my prayers. . . .
For I had much joy and consolation in thy love,
because the hearts of the saints have been refreshed
by thee, brother.'

What
prompts
Thanks
here.
The following, then, is the course of thought :
Philemon's Christian love, growing out of his faith
in Christ, had manifested itself in active beneficence,
by which so many brethren were helped and cheered.

116

Good Occasion for Thanks

The vivid and sympathetic apprehension of this had **Philemon** 4-7. infused a happy glow of joy and comfort into the apostle's own bosom; and this in turn had kindled into a flame of grateful emotion toward God for having wrought these graces in Philemon, and into the special prayer that all Christian good might flow back again into Philemon's own soul.

What a chain of happy influences this verse commemorates! It sounds like a chord in heaven's own music. For what can be the song of the better world but the prolongation of this triple note on a higher key? Great joy in the heart, drawing its inspiration from the presence and power of love, and uttering itself in outbursts of praise and holy desire unto God! This is the very joy that swells in the bosom of angels.

Is it not pleasant to find the apostle writing of his joy and comfort in such untoward circumstances as those in which he was now placed as a prisoner? It reminds us of our blessed Saviour's words about His own joy when standing within the very shadow of His cross. ' These things have I spoken unto you, **John xv. 11.** that My joy might remain in you, and that your joy might be full.'

How is it the apostle writes in such a sunny, Paul's sunny Spirit. blessed way? It did not spring from any pleasant environments in his earthly lot, nor from an easy-going and naturally light-hearted temperament. This is a world where grave and earnest spirits are needed much; and Paul was one of them. His was the solemnity, his the occasional sadness, incident to all profound thought and feeling; his

The Epistle of St Paul to Philemon

Philemon
4-7. was the burden of deep, loving sympathy, which shares the sorrows of others, and carries the weight of the world's best interests. Nor was he permitted to bask in the sunshine of prosperity. Many have to struggle with oppressive difficulties and multiplied trials. And Paul again was one of these.

What with his weakened and relaxed nervous condition, what with frequent loneliness and isolation, his heart aching under disappointment or lacerated by the desertion of false friends, what with 'stripes and imprisonment,' weariness and watching, poverty, humiliation or danger, and, above all, what with pitiful misconception of his meanings and motives, how much, like his master, he was made 'acquainted with grief.' But he is none the less conscious of an inward cheerfulness that refuses to be overclouded. 'As sorrowing, yet alway rejoicing,' is his motto still.

The Secret of it.   The secret of all this 'joy and consolation' is found in his spirit of mingled gratitude and benevolence. A thankless heart has no security for any abiding joy and consolation ; no more has a selfish heart. We read of Robert Hall (Olinthus Gregory's edition of his works, vol. i. p. 136, with note) : 'He uniformly retired from the social meetings with the humbler members of his flock, full of grateful references to the pleasure he had felt—emphatically saying, ' It was very pleasant. I enjoyed it. I enjoy everything.' Here was a man whose powers seemed almost adapted for converse with disembodied spirits—whose thoughts were frequently wandering through eternity—a man, too, whose

life was a constant wrestling against bodily anguish **Philemon**
—whose corporeal structure was an apparatus of **4-7.**
torture—and yet who was able to seek and find
delight among the humbler recreations of society,
and to exclaim, in the gratitude and fulness of his
heart: ' I enjoy everything.' . . . Hall, on the rack
of a diseased organisation, is able to enjoy everything. Byron, when his temples are throbbing with
the self-inflicted pains of a vicious life, cries out:
' There is nothing but misery in this world, I think.'
If this contrast does not speak to the hearts and
understandings of men, the voice of wisdom would
be heard in vain from the jaws of the sepulchre
itself.'

' I had much joy and consolation in thy love,
because the hearts of the saints have been refreshed
by thee, brother '; and I do thank and praise God
for all the good He has wrought in thee and through
thee.'

He rejoiced because of all the love which Philemon **For Love's**
had been enabled to show. He was grateful to God **Sake.**
for implanting in him such a spirit, and causing it to
produce such kindly fruits. These fruits were not,
indeed, reaped by the apostle himself; but so
thoroughly could he identify the interests of others
with his own, that he felt a pleasure in Philemon's
charitable services, and was overflowingly grateful
and happy at the disposition on his part to render
them to others.

The very thought of many hearts being relieved
and cheered sent a thrill of devout satisfaction into
Paul's own heart. ' I had much joy and consolation,'

The Epistle of St Paul to Philemon

Philemon
4-7. he says, with a sort of double emphasis; the 'joy' having reference to his sense of happy delight, and the 'consolation' to the comfort and support thereby afforded him in his distress.

And is not this what we chiefly need in this world of sorrow and suffering—a joy that shall afford consolation? With the joy of amusement or of prosperity, and the like, we may dispense, but not with this, if we would have a guarantee of inward comfort. Yet how can it be secured? We must find joy in love—in love experienced by us, in love exercised by us; 'I had much joy in thy love, because the hearts of saints are refreshed by thee.' So it is that,—

> 'All other joys go less
> To the one joy of doing kindnesses.'

Vulgar Joy. He will never want for supplies of joy and consolation who finds a great delight in love manifested by others or enjoyed by them; who, free from envy, takes an exalted pleasure in the gifts and graces of others, and who, ever on the outlook for occasions to be thankful, is willing to regard as mercies to himself what are blessings to others. The vulgar joy of earth would snatch at everything for itself; but the divinely beautiful disposition of being happy in the diffusion of happiness grows radiant with a sunshine akin to the Divine blessedness itself.

Blessedness of a beneficent Spirit. If any one go after his own personal joy and comfort with an all-consuming and self-seeking eagerness, he may as well think to get the rainbow by chasing it. Here we would remind the reader how thoroughly one like Mr. J. S. Mill is forced to

Good Occasion for Thanks

surrender his whole philosophical theory of life, and **Philemon** 4-7. lapses into hopeless inconsistency, when in one sentence he says, 'I never, indeed, wavered in the conviction that happiness is the test of all rules of conduct and the end of life;' and yet in the third sentence after this he adds: 'The only chance is to treat, not happiness, but some end external to it, as the purpose of life.' Strange contradiction! Personal happiness the great end of life, yet not to be dealt with as this directly!—Certainly, to be absorbed in our own private comfort, and pursue it for itself, is ever and invariably to fare like the man who in his See singular passage in his *Auto-biography*, pp. 141, 142. foolish over-anxiety to catch a delicate creature alive, suddenly puts his foot on it, and finds it just dying when he gets it in his hands. Ah! how different the experience of the self-denying and beneficent spirit! 'I had much joy in thy love, because the hearts of the saints have been refreshed by thee, *brother,*' the apostle very touchingly adds, in token of his kindly and *fraternal* feeling to Philemon, in recalling his acts of benevolence. This joy in love for love's sake is more than happiness. It is blessedness, the guarantee and security of happiness. For as the word indicates, happiness looks rather to what we *have*, but blessedness rather to what we *are.*

THE BODY OF THE EPISTLE

I

APPROACHING THE SUBJECT

PHILEMON verses 8, 9

WHEREFORE, though having much confidence in Christ to enjoin on thee what is becoming, yet, for love's sake, I beseech rather—being such an one as Paul, an old man, and now also a prisoner of Jesus Christ.

Philemon 8, 9. WHEN the apostle had made up his mind to interpose on behalf of Onesimus, two courses were open to him. He might have written in a tone of authority, or of simple persuasiveness. He could have enjoined: he prefers to entreat:

'Such ever was love's way
To rise, it stoops.'

Nor will his beseechings prove less effectual than any words of command, in stripping Philemon of resentment towards his bondman.

In the fable, the colder the north wind blew, the closer the traveller drew his cloak about him; but when the sun stole out with fervent heat, how ready he was to cast it off. How irritating is all ill-timed display of authority! How provocative of resistance an unseasonable sharpness of tone! The chill breath of unbrotherly words might have steeled Philemon's heart and made him hug more closely to him the cloak of his resentful feelings.

Approaching the Subject

The apostle is alive to the importance not only of Philemon 8, 9. what he says, but of how he says it. Much depends on his setting all to the right key by 'speaking the truth *in love*.' Ministering the Truth in Love.

He will not, therefore, assume an authoritative tone. He would not crush with dictatorial argument even :

> 'Who overcomes by force,
> Hath overcome but half his foe.'

He will not drive with peremptory threats. He will win Philemon with persuasion.

This is peculiarly consonant to the spirit of the Gospel. 'We persuade men.' 'By winning words we conquer willing hearts' (Milton). Does not God Himself condescend to plead His cause with sinners, saying 'Come now, let us reason together'? (Isaiah l. 18). We are ambassadors for Christ *as though God* 2 Cor. v. 20. *did beseech you by us*: we pray you in Christ's stead, be ye reconciled to God.' This is the tone of Gospel-mercy :

> 'Casting on the dark her gracious bow,
> And evermore beseeching men with tears
> And earnest sighs, to hear, believe, and live.'

The apostle, however, does not forget, nor allow Philemon to forget, who it is that pleads. He is not insensible to the fact of his apostleship, nor the grave responsibilities such a position represents. 'Having much confidence in Christ;' or, 'having full authority in Christ to enjoin on thee what is becoming.'

The words 'in Christ' indicate that apostleship

The Epistle of St Paul to Philemon

Philemon 8, 9. was, in Paul's view, a solemn trust more than a personal dignity. This preserves him from the un-bending haughtiness of the mere official 'dressed in a little brief authority,' no less than from the equally offensive pride that 'apes humility.' He will not depreciate, and will take care that others do not despise, the sacred office with which he is invested. He confidently asserts its rights, and his own call and fitness in Christ to exercise them.

Apostleship a Trust not Dignity only.

Paul waives his Right. He has authority to command in all matters of Christian faith and practice. The present is a case where he has a right to apply the law of Christ, and might peremptorily enjoin what is convenient (or rather, what is morally becoming and Christianly befitting; the word 'convenient,' in the authorised version, signifying here not 'what suits our purpose,' which is all it means now, but 'what is proper or becoming in a moral sense,' which was its earlier though now obsolete usage). He is hinting at the forgiveness and kind reception of Onesimus, which he might command as a duty. But he waives that right, and prefers to entreat.

And why? He assigns three reasons; and the frankness with which the apostle does it is ex-ceedingly winning, apart from the weight of the reasons themselves. Here 'grace' as well as 'truth' is 'poured into his lips.' He can waive his rights without detracting anything from them.

His three-fold Reasons. There is a central reason, 'for love's sake,'—and this is flanked by reasons of a personal kind on either side—one introduced by the word 'wherefore,' having reference to Philemon's disposition, and the

124

other, 'being such an one,' having reference to Paul's own disposition.

When the apostle says, 'for love's sake,' he is speaking of the principle of Christian love at large, not of any particular application of it, like Philemon's love for Paul, or Paul's love for Philemon, but generally. 'Having due respect to the claims of love, I beseech you.' And he is the more willing to let entreaty guide his pen, as he has every reason to think that Philemon will not be backward to respond to a loving appeal.

This is the force of the 'wherefore.' It reflects back on the previous verses, to those parts especially which showed that Philemon was not deficient in this element of love. 'I have heard of thy love for all the saints : I had much joy and consolation in thy love, because the hearts of saints have been refreshed by thee, brother :' *wherefore* I feel I may approach you on behalf of a poor saint with the higher considerations which love suggests, rather than with the exactions which lawful authority might impose.

Philemon must have felt exceedingly gratified at being thus addressed. Paul meant him to feel so. For there is not only a pleasure, but a quickening power in a few words of kindly commendation from the lips of sincerity.

Paul, therefore, likes to praise wherever he can. Even in writing to those churches where he had much to censure, he seeks occasion to commend as far as faithfulness will allow. His is far from the fault-finding spirit, that waspishly fastens on blemishes with eager satisfaction.

125

The Epistle of St Paul to Philemon

Philemon
8, 9.
Paul's recognition of all that is good in Philemon, is an admirable example to Philemon to recognise all the good Paul had found in Onesimus. Pleading continually in prayer for you, I wish now to plead with you.

Ever excel
Thyself.
The implied compliment in the 'wherefore' is thus a very delicate one; but there is no flattery about it. Heavenly grace, not earthly art, has invented it. By cordially acknowledging Philemon's excellences the apostle desires to call them forth into further exercise; his brotherly love he means especially to turn to practical account on behalf of Onesimus. He knows that a hearty 'Well done!' will be a spur to his doing better and excelling his former self. There is a something of the world, a something half heathenish in urging a man just to excel others; but it is a heavenly and Christian thing to prompt a man to excel himself and surpass even his own previous best.

The other reason for waiving authority and choosing to entreat, is found in Paul's own disposition : 'I rather beseech,' or, as we may put it, 'I like better to beseech.' It suits my nature. It accords with my present mood and inclination. Not the weakness of my case, but my special interest in it, prompts my appealing tone. Not outward pressure, but inward affection, brings me to you as a suppliant. To beseech is best adapted to both a service and a feeling of love.

Beseeching
best
expresses
Love.
The apostle, having stated his reasons for entreating, goes on to indicate why his entreaty should be carefully regarded. The expression 'being such an

one' should, according to the best authorities, be **Philemon** made to refer to what precedes, and be therefore **8, 9.** slightly detached from what follows, occupying a separate place of its own ; thus :

Wherefore, though having much boldness (or consciousness of authority) in Christ to enjoin on thee what is becoming, yet for love's sake I like better to beseech; being so minded, I do, as Paul an old man, and now also in bonds for Christ, beseech thee earnestly for one whom I now commend to thee.

We do not understand him as making an appeal to Philemon's pity and commiseration, but as lending a pathetic and dignified validity to his request that should entitle it to the most respectful consideration. Something was due to the Christian temper of the apostle, in that he would not stand on his peculiar rights as an apostle—he would do nothing through vain-glory, because he 'had a regard to the things of others.' So would he have Philemon ready to forgo, if not some of his legal rights at least some of his powers as a master.

To be appealed to by one who has a conscious **Beseeching** right to enjoin, but who out of loving considerations **best _wins_ Love.** prefers to plead, is an argument in itself of consummate force in the case, even before its merits have been reached.

But if the pleader be Paul, the friend whom Philemon knows well, and to whom he owes so much, is not something more due from him to the very name that has such hallowed memories and precious associations connected with it in his mind ?

The Epistle of St Paul to Philemon

Philemon 8, 9. If, in addition to this, Paul be now getting old, should not years inspire respect for any entreaty, especially if they be years of service, of unbroken friendship, or of high spiritual status?

And finally, if it be Christ's suffering servant that pleads, what can be denied? and who can turn an indifferent ear to the request of one with such sacred claims to the most respectful regard? Not Philemon surely. He felt, doubtless, what we feel —irresistibly subdued by the mingled grace and dignity with which the apostle approaches his subject.

II

PAUL UNVEILING THE SUBJECT

PHILEMON verses 9-12

BEING such an one (I do), as Paul, an old man, and now also a prisoner of Jesus Christ, beseech thee for my child, whom I have begotten in my bonds, Onesimus; who in time past was to thee unprofitable, but now is profitable to thee and to me: whom I have sent back to thee; HIM (receive as myself), that is, mine own flesh.

Philemon 9-12. THE intensity of feeling under which the apostle writes is very apparent from the repetition of the strong word *beseech*. 'For love's sake, I *beseech*' (ver. 9). '*I beseech* thee for my child' (ver. 10).

Feeling controlled by Judgment. But he does not allow his feelings to overmaster his judgment. They will give a glow to his language, and they will breathe into his words what shall avail to melt the heart of Philemon; but their **very** warmth will only help to put him on ways of marshalling his pleadings with greatest effect.

128

Paul Unveiling the Subject

He has already let Philemon know that he is **Philemon** about to make an important, it may be even a hard **9-12.** request of him; but before he can venture to tell him what it is or whom it concerns he must bring him into a susceptible and acquiescent mood.

With what address therefore he throws himself **Real Love** in between master and servant for a little, that **includes** **Wisdom.** he may have an opportunity of moving the sympathies of Philemon by a few touching personal allusions. 'As Paul, an old man, and now also a prisoner of Jesus Christ, I beseech thee.'

By such a stroke of tenderest pathos he cannot but have smitten from Philemon's heart a gush of genuine feeling. Touched as he already was with the honour of a letter from Paul direct; grateful for the warm and generous words of commendation he had just read, and not unmoved by the friendly remembrances with which he had been greeted, it is surely no fancy to think of a tear-drop gathering in his eye as he felt the subduing influence of such a style of address from such a man.

The thought of old times brought up afresh by **Touches** the very name of Paul; the tender memories of all **deepest** **Chords.** the past and the singular kindliness of the apostle to him at present; the image of the glorious veteran getting old and worn out in the Master's service; the knowledge of his own spiritual father lying in bonds for the sake of Christ—how should Philemon not have been melted even to tears! How should he not have been inwardly saying, 'What can such an one as Paul ask, and I refuse? Let me but hear his wish that I may do it.'

The Epistle of St Paul to Philemon

**Philemon
9-12.**

But it does not suit the apostle's purpose to withdraw too suddenly from before Onesimus, whom he still gently withholds from view. '*I beseech thee for my child.*' Then it is not for himself he pleads. 'That is so like the apostle!' might be the reflection of Philemon. And yet it is some one very near and dear to him—' my child ' implies so close and peculiar a relationship.

Is nobly benevolent.

Philemon doubtless understands it as referring to some beloved convert whom Paul would commend to his sympathy and aid. And before he is aware, his mind is probably occupied with benevolent designs on behalf of one so favourably introduced to his notice : he will attend to his wants and his welfare. He will do this the more cheerfully as he learns with greater clearness from the next words, 'whom I have begotten in my bonds,' how specially tender is the tie that knits this convert to the apostle.

Ah! what wisdom, what holy art in the pleader, to put in the forefront these thrilling announcements —the very turning-point and triumph of the case— the pith and substance of all his pleadings—before he introduces the offender's name.

This keeping of Philemon in suspense as long as possible, has ever been regarded as a stroke of consummate skill.

Is skilful in pleading.

Paul takes care that the offender shall not be mentioned till he shall have contrived in a word or two of rhetorical power to lift Philemon into a relenting mood—and only then will he usher the obnoxious bondsman into the immediate notice of

Paul Unveiling the Subject

his master. 'He for whom I intercede is a Christian convert, and like yourself, one of my own : he is my Benjamin, "a son of my right hand," and, more than all, he is a Benoni, "a son of my sorrow," for whom I have travailed in birth while in bonds and imprisonment : and his name ' (only now it comes out, in the midst of such gracious associations) 'is— ONESIMUS.'

What a surprise to Philemon! Perhaps what a revulsion of feeling in him for a few moments! perchance a little natural anger, possibly a measure of suspicion and incredulity, even some vexation and bitterness!

But Paul has provided for any such tumult of contending emotions. He hastens first of all by a frank recognition of the shortcomings of Onesimus, and by an assurance of his penitence and amendment, to appease the master and soothe his ruffled mind. 'Who in time past was to thee unprofitable, but now is profitable to thee, and to me.'

'Unprofitable once on a time '—this is a form of acknowledgment more mild but not less accurate than 'unfaithful,' 'injurious,' or similar more severe phrases which Paul is careful to avoid, lest he might inflame the already somewhat sore and irritated sensibilities of Philemon.

But Paul seems to have had special reasons for choosing these particular words here ; and we must not miss the delicate stroke of something like good-humour or pleasantry to which for a moment the apostle unbends. The name of Onesimus was not an ill-omened one. It means 'profitable and

The Epistle of St Paul to Philemon

serviceable.' Why not turn this little circumstance if possible to account? If by taking advantage of what the name suggests, Paul could only get Philemon to relax the severity of his countenance and make a sunny gleam chase the frown from his brow, much would be gained. 'I beseech thee for Onesimus, once, it must be allowed, not very much of a servant to you, but now a servant indeed both to you and to me.'

Paul felt it difficult to introduce the unsavoury name; but by an easy and affectionate allusion to its meaning, he both helps to drown its disagreeable memories, and surprises Philemon out of his worst resentments.

To indulge in any jest at so serious a moment as this would have been impolitic in the extreme. But there is a world of difference between an inconsiderate joke and a touch of geniality, as much as between the coarse laugh and the smile that is brimful of benignity.

A stiff manner is chilling, and often proves excessively awkward at some critical juncture. It was just such a trying moment the apostle has to face, where a little dexterous tact may alter the whole aspect of things, enabling the writer to turn a corner and so relieve the situation. With what felicity he has done it is patent to all, especially as he hastens to add the material circumstance, 'Whom I have sent back to thee.'

If the word 'unprofitable' showed that Paul had not been imposed on by Onesimus with any plausible tale, but had learned the whole truth of his mis-

132

Paul Unveiling the Subject

Philemon 9-12.

conduct—which would at once allay all evil surmisings that were apt to occur to Philemon's mind—the fact of his being sent back caused matters to assume a very satisfactory appearance. 'The letter is not meant to prescribe terms to me ; or to make a bargain with me beforehand on behalf of the renegade, as the condition of his return. He is actually here, trusting himself to my generosity!' 'In time past was to thee unprofitable, but now is profitable to thee and to me: whom I have sent back to thee.'

There is more than winning geniality in these announcements of the apostle. These are unimpeachable testimonies to the reality of Onesimus' penitence, and the practical value of his religion.

A real Penitent.

Wherever true godliness exists it enhances the worth of earthly service. Bond-work is at best by no means very profitable. Indeed, as of all forms of service it is the lowest and the least removed from that of the brute creation, so it is the least capable of yielding increase. Slavery is, in short, economically a mistake. And where the bondman works in the *spirit* of the system, which is one of compulsion and terrorism, the natural result is still worse.

The drawbacks of Slavery.

'God fixed it certain that whatever day
Makes man a slave, takes half his worth away.'

Idleness and escape by flight are morally inseparable from forced labour. And if the system go so far as to say to the bondman, 'You have no rights,' he may consistently retort, 'Then I have no responsibilities either.'

In this sense all bond-service is comparatively

133

The Epistle of St Paul to Philemon

'unprofitable.' But it was not to this the apostle here immediately alludes. He wished simply to indicate that one who absconded like Onesimus could hardly be pointed to as an exemplary specimen of good and hearty service.

Love is courteous and deferential.

Now, however, he is changed for the better. Being supplied with religious principle and animated with ennobling motives, his life will be pervaded by a new and improved spirit. The *man* was raised. His *service* will rise with him. Paul had found it so. He 'now is profitable to thee and to me : whom I have sent back to thee : him (receive as myself), that is, mine own flesh.' We must note the refined deference paid just at this critical point to Philemon. It is seen in the repetition of the '*thee*' three times in rapid succession, while the next verse begins with 'thou.' The same consideration seems to have dictated the peculiar transposition of 'thee' and 'me.'

According to the ordinary law of Greek and Latin arrangement, the first person should precede the second. But instead of 'me and thee,' it is 'thee and me,' Philemon having thus an unwonted precedence. There is a nice touch of courtesy in all this, which would not be thrown away on Paul's correspondent.

What the apostle wishes for Onesimus he does not yet divulge. It is not expressed till the 17th verse—so many things crowd on him for utterance, and such is the intensity of his thoughts and feelings, that he must relieve his mind of some of them before resuming the interrupted thread.

Paul Unveiling the Subject

But then with what force the request is at last introduced! It is indeed evident enough, without his saying it in so many words, that he desires forgiveness and favourable reception for the offender; but how much more, or how much this should include, remains to be seen.

Meanwhile it is enough so to have introduced the name of Onesimus as to have disarmed the master's animosity, and prevented any unseemly outbreak of passion and violence.

'No procedure is so apt to gain a hearing,' says **Delicacy of** Chrysostom, with equal shrewdness and neatness, **true Love.** 'as not to ask for everything at once.' It is sufficient to have presented the claims of the bondman so as to have caught the sympathy of Philemon and worked upon his heart.

If the Lord has met and has forgiven the servant, can he remain unforgiven of his master? If Onesimus be Paul's child, what less can Philemon do than reflect the apostle's happy feelings, as if he should say, 'For this my son was dead, and is alive again; he was lost, and is found.' Him, adds the apostle, with great fervour, who is 'mine own flesh,' dear to me as my very soul.

The Epistle of St Paul to Philemon

III

PAUL EXPLAINING THE SUBJECT

PHILEMON verses 13, 14.

WHOM I would have retained with me, that in thy stead he might minister unto me in the bonds of the Gospel : but without thine assent would I do nothing ; that thy service should not be as it were of necessity, but willingly.

Philemon 13, 14.
Two possible Misconceptions.

IN thinking of the apostle sending Onesimus back to Philemon, we must guard against two opposite misapprehensions.

We are not, on the one hand, to suppose that Paul returned him against the bondman's own will; nor, on the other hand, that he sent him back under protest, as if he denied Philemon's claims to his service. In fact, it was not a civil power he exercised at all, but a simple pastoral conciliation. Let the words speak for themselves: 'Whom I have sent back to thee : him (that is) my own flesh.' Rather different this in tone from that of compulsion !

The apostle did not admit the master's right to deal with the bondman as he pleased ; and the bare thought of maltreatment was nothing short of personal agony. He is my own flesh : receive him as myself : no longer as a servant, but above a servant, a brother beloved, in the flesh and in the Lord.

Yet, in the face of such expressions, this act of the apostle has been sometimes pleaded as a sanction for inflicting penalties on any who would not thrust a slave back on his bondage.

Such a misconception of the apostle's spirit is

Paul Explaining the Subject

as transparent as it is happily antiquated. The Philemon 13, 14. humane arrangements of the old Hebrew code were too deeply engraven on his memory. 'Thou shalt Deut. xxiii. 15, 16. not deliver unto his master the servant which is escaped from his master unto thee: he shall dwell with thee, even among you, in that place which he shall choose in one of thy gates, where it liketh him best: *thou shalt not oppress him.*'

But while the apostle guards and defines the servant's rights, he will not usurp or interfere with the master's prerogatives. Like the Lord Luke xii. 13-15. Himself in a similar case, he refuses to act as a judge or magistrate on a question of secular jurisdiction.

He declines, as a religious teacher, to trench on the functions of the civil ruler, or to usurp the duties and responsibilities of the master. He proceeds simply to expound the Christian principles involved in the case, and to act upon them himself; leaving Philemon to apply them also on his side, under a sense of accountability to the Lord.

So far as Paul's personal liking and convenience Apostle's attachment to Onesimus. were concerned, he could have wished very much to keep Onesimus beside him, so attached had he become to the bondman, and so useful had he found him. 'Whom I would have retained with me, that in thy stead he might minister unto me in the bonds of the gospel.'

With much delicacy, the apostle assumes that Philemon would gladly perform many kind offices to himself personally for Christ's sake, if he had the opportunity—a sentiment to which Philemon

The Epistle of St Paul to Philemon

Philemon
13, 14. would cordially respond. The idea of Onesimus, however, standing as his substitute, and being thought qualified to fill his place towards the apostle ('in thy stead he might,' etc.) may not have been so welcome. 'See the power of the gospel,' says Theodoret, forcibly; 'it has set the slave on a level with the master.'

But the very fact that Paul could be so complimentary to Onesimus would serve still further to convince Philemon how estimable the slave-convert had become. The services which the apostle contemplated him as specially qualified to render were probably of a varied character.

When he says, 'that in thy stead he might minister unto me in the bonds of the gospel,' the main reference is doubtless to the innumerable personal offices which a prisoner like himself, hampered and crippled by untoward restraints in his work, required for ordinary comfort and convenience, and for which he was dependent on some trusty friend, willing to make himself generally useful. The idea is not that of a mere body-servant, but of a devoted helper, whose qualifications (whatever they were) might be utilised to their fullest extent in every serviceable way.

Onesimus a
help. Though Onesimus were a bondman, we are not to think of him as necessarily destitute of educational attainments; for slaves were not debarred from means of instruction, and many of them in Rome and elsewhere were of distinguished ability and literary acquirement. We are not precluded, therefore, from conceiving of Onesimus aiding the

138

Paul Explaining the Subject

apostle in many different ways, and even taking **Philemon** **13, 14.** part in evangelistic labours uuder his immediate direction.

But, however serviceable it would be to have the grateful convert at his bidding, other considerations of primary moment led the apostle to sacrifice his inclinations and convenience.

A profound proverb tells us that ' In matters of Why he parts with him. duty, first thoughts are best : in matters of prudence, second thoughts are best.' Here they both combine in leading to the same result. I would have retained Onesimus : but I would not run counter to the great principle that a service or favour must be spontaneous and unconstrained, to be acceptable and morally praiseworthy. 'Without thine assent would I do nothing; that thy service should not be as it were of necessity, but willingly ;' that is, should not seem to be extorted, but truly voluntary.

Paul had good reason to believe that Philemon would not at all object to Onesimus being employed as he had just hinted; but the master's consent coming only after the services had been rendered, would look as if it had been extorted—Philemon not having a choice beforehand of approving or disapproving. Paul could not continue to use the servant's labours without the master's knowledge, and yet reckon them as favours shown him by the master himself.

See here Paul's abhorrence of enforced or con- No liking for forced Service. strained service. What a hard blow he deals at the whole system of involuntary servitude! What a dislike and suspicion he has at everything that savours

139

The Epistle of St Paul to Philemon

of exaction, where free consent beforehand has not
been secured!

We may therefore readily conclude that he proceeded on the same principle with Onesimus as he
avows he had adopted towards Philemon. 'Not by
constraint, but willingly.' This is the fundamental
principle of all service worthy of the name of
service.

No doubt the bondman had risks to face in returning to his master. But Paul would hail and foster
his wish to go back and repair the wrongs he had
certainly done to Philemon. For it is a cardinal
virtue of Christian morality, that while in many cases
it is enough for a man to confess his sins to God
alone, this will not suffice where injury has been
done to any fellow-creature. An indisposition to
make all possible amends and render ample satisfaction would argue a serious defect in repentance, if
not throw suspicion on its reality altogether.

Christian
Magnan-
imity.

Not often, however, can the rectitude of Christian
principle be seen gilded with a more radiant glory
than when we witness Paul and Onesimus submitting
for its sake to all the sacrifices and hazards it may
entail. Such an example of Christian magnanimity
can hardly fail to evoke a kindred spirit in the
master. They have done justly: what else remains
but that he should show mercy?

Seldom can Christian charity seem more like an
angel from heaven than when, with the tear-drop of
compassion and entreaty in its eye, and with the
protection afforded to the humble penitent by the
covert of its wing, it strives, as Paul does here, to

reconcile estranged hearts and knit them together in everlasting bonds.

IV

PAUL ARGUING THE SUBJECT

PHILEMON verse 15.

For perhaps to this end he departed for a season, that thou shouldest receive him to thyself for ever.

In persuading Philemon to deal considerately with Onesimus, the apostle proceeds to bring into view the *providential* aspects of the case; 'For perhaps to this end he departed for a season, that thou shouldest receive him to thyself for ever; no longer as a bondman, but above a bondman, a brother beloved.'

This assigns a further reason which induced Paul to send Onesimus back to his master: I send him back again, in order to give you an opportunity to deal with him according to the true nature of the relationship in which he now stands before you—*for* perhaps it was for this very purpose of being set in a new and improved relationship to you that he was permitted, in God's providence, to depart for a time from your service.   Good at least has come out of it, not intended by the fugitive, indeed, but brought about by a merciful Providence.

An overruling Providence.

The great idea underlying the present turn of thought is, that in every event of life, good or bad, God has not only an interest, but a meaning or purpose through it, all His own.   There is not merely a general superintendence of Providence over

141

The Epistle of St Paul to Philemon

Philemon
15. the affairs of men, but a Providential agency at work in the very midst of them.

Very different, no doubt, is the Divine agency from the human, with which it mysteriously mingles. Divine and human Agencies. Not more distinct is the Lord of all from the works of His own hands, than is His providential government distinct from what it regulates; yet moving Distinct yet interlacing. freely in the midst of His creation, He no less freely interlaces human agencies with. His own.

Man's history, in short, is not the mere sum of his own thoughts and doings, any more than the well-compacted web is the mere sum of the weft-threads shot across its range—there are the slowly unrolling warp-threads as well; and not less surely is there the unfolding of a providential agency to bind into one the crossing and recrossing lines of human activity.

Hence we continually see results issuing from trivial matters which the actors in them never contemplated:

'A Divinity that shapes our Ends.'
> 'And that should teach us
> There's a Divinity that shapes our ends
> Rough-hew them how we will.'

But the special feature in Divine Providence on which the apostle's argument proceeds is the fact that God brings good out of man's evil.

Over how many incidents of human experience may not the saying of Joseph to his brethren be verified: 'As for you, ye thought evil against me; but God meant it unto good, . . . to save much Judges xiv. 14. people alive,' or the riddle of Samson, as interpreting Divine Providence, 'Out of the eater came forth meat, and out of the strong' (or *tainted* carcase)

142

Paul Arguing the Subject

'came forth sweetness;' exemplified in his own Philemon exploits, in which he took occasion against the 15. Philistines, but the Lord took occasion to deliver Israel. This principle is exemplified most vividly at God's the cross. The very climax of human wickedness— purpose seen at the the crucifixion of the Lord of glory—becomes the Cross. method for cancelling and obliterating the sins of men. 'And so, albeit the actors in Christ's death wickedly intended nothing but to show their hatred and testify their envy, yet God brought another matter out of their malice, and made His endless mercy to man appear in His work of redemption. God would have Christ die: Caiaphus would have Him die: Pilate would have Him die: Judas and the Jews would have Him die: but God for our redemption, they for other ends, as Judas for covet- Attersoll's ousness, the priests for envy, and Pilate to please the *Philemon*, people.' p. 296.

So Paul would have Philemon mark how God had Evoking educed good out of evil in the present instance. The Good out of conversion of Onesimus had been the issue of his Evil. flight from Colosse. This had never entered into his own original design at all, nor did it in the least degree lessen the wickedness of his conduct. But as the event had turned out entirely different from all human purpose, we must recognise in it a merciful Divine ordering, whatever interpretation we may put on the further design of God in having thus graciously overruled the misconduct of Onesimus.

The apostle writes with reverent caution of the Divine purposes—for while God has His own meanings in everything, He alone can certainly declare

The Epistle of St Paul to Philemon

them in any case. As therefore it would be rash to pronounce decisively, and as absolute certainty is not necessary to the force of the apostle's plea, he contents

A reverent 'perhaps.'

himself with a judicious 'perhaps:' I send him back; 'for *perhaps* to this end he departed for a season, that thou shouldest receive him to thyself for ever.'

The 'perhaps' does not belong to the word 'departed,' but to what follows: not, 'perhaps he departed,' for he actually departed; but 'he departed for a season, perhaps to this end, that thou mightest have him back with thee for ever.' As God took occasion to bring unmistakable good out of the bondman's departure, may it not very well be also that He brought this about that you should secure the opportunity of doing good to the man, as God Himself had done; and that I should take occasion to afford you the opportunity, by sending him to you; so that you may receive him no longer in the light of a mere bondman, but what he has really become, a brother beloved? I would on no account like to stand in the way of your so dealing with him, and therefore I send him.

The apostle by no means suggests that is the sole or chief design of God's providence. There were doubtless many merciful purposes in the case:

'In human works though laboured on with pain,
A thousand movements scarce one object gain;
In God's, a single movement may its end produce,
And serve to further too some other use.'

Illustrated in John Wiclif.

Let us take an outstanding historical illustration of this principle of the Divine procedure. In the fourteenth century, Urban VI. and Clement VII.

presented the scandalous spectacle of each claiming **Philemon**
papal power, and in the exercise of it excommunica- 15.
ting one another. At this crisis John Wiclif was
busy with his translation of Scripture: and it was
mainly owing to the confusions which arose from the
papal schism that he was left so free to prosecute
his great reforms.

For many ends, doubtless, was that singular schism
divinely intended—perhaps to pour contempt on the
recent dogma of a pope's personal infallibility when
acting officially, and perhaps to afford the needful
unmolested security to Wiclif and his work; this
having been certainly one of its immediate and
palpable results.

But Philemon could never be wrong in following
any suggestion to good.

As, therefore, the event had turned out well, how
could Philemon give way to any thoughts of ill?

The force of the appeal is enhanced by the language
in which Paul takes care to clothe it. He says
'departed,' not 'fled' or 'escaped': he would use
no word that might awaken resentful feeling in the
master; and he therefore chooses one that describes
not the quality of the servant's act, but simply its
external aspect.

He departed for a season (for an hour, as the **Appeasing**
original mildly puts it)—Philemon being deprived of **Considera-tions.**
his services for a short time, after all—an appeasing
consideration, not as if it had been for many years.
Exactly how long we are not told: it was a brief
period at most.

And finally, He was parted from thee for a little

**Philemon
15.**

while, that thou mightest receive him; possess his full and real self without any drawback: thus he directs attention to the great gain accruing to Philemon; as if he should say, 'Hitherto you had only *his service,* now you are to have *himself;* his heart is toward you in the bonds of a relationship that makes him all your own, and for all time to come. Through human perversity you lost a slave; but through Divine mercy and grace you gain a brother.'

Thus, by bringing into prominence the present or providential situation of matters, and by dwelling on what Onesimus now is rather than on what he was, the apostle would cool the heat of Philemon's resentment, and prevent it from kindling into inflamed personal or private passion.

**Case of
Joseph.**

The resemblance of this plea to the lovely one in Joseph's address to his brethren has been recognised by successive expositors. If he had allowed his mind to dwell on the wrongs his brothers had done him—if he had brooded on their unnatural behaviour in selling him for a slave, on their previous cruel treatment of him, and on all their neglect of anything like brotherly love, how could he have smothered the uprisings of bitter retaliation?

What enabled him to adopt the melting accents of tender love to his brothers, both at the earlier interview, when he made himself known to them, and afterwards at Jacob's death, when their old sin rose again to put them in new terror? How did he gain so great a victory over himself, without a thought of ever 'nursing his wrath, to keep it warm?'

146

Paul Arguing the Subject

How but by looking steadfastly at God's gracious **Philemon** providence in overruling their treachery, and turning **15.** it, unwittingly to them, into an occasion of blessing? 'Now therefore be not grieved, nor angry with yourselves, that ye sold me hither: for God did send me before you to preserve life.' 'But as for **Gen. xlv. 5.** you, ye thought evil against me; but God meant it unto good. . . . And he comforted them, and spake kindly unto them.' **Gen. l. 20, 21.**

So would Paul preserve Philemon from the snare of magnifying his own grievances, and would teach him never to upbraid nor reproach a penitent brother about wicked courses he has forsaken.

It is easy enough to feel cool and indifferent about evil where we are not hurt; but it is another matter to forbear and forgive where we have been personally affronted and wronged.

Only they who 'follow God as dear children' will conspire with the leadings of Divine Providence to welcome back the sinner, without abating any righteous indignation against his sin. For the holiest are ever the most patient to the bad: the purest are the tenderest: those who are most sensitive about wickedness, and whose souls most easily fire up and tingle with burning disapprobation of evil, are ever foremost to show mercy to the evil-doer. And they who best obey the first part of the precept, 'Be not overcome of evil,' are they who best discharge the other part, 'Overcome evil with good.'

The Epistle of St Paul to Philemon

V

PAUL PLEADING THE SUBJECT

PHILEMON verse 16.

No longer as a bondman, but above a bondman, a brother beloved, especially to me, but how much more to thee, both in the flesh, and in the Lord?

Philemon 16.

A Fulcrum and Lever.

'GIVE me a fulcrum on which to plant my lever,' said the ancient geometer, 'and I will move the world.'

In the few and simple words of direction that now come before us, we shall find a fulcrum and a lever both—as firm a fulcrum and as powerful a lever as have ever been brought into operation for lifting into a higher plane the whole world of social existence.

Here, too, we are permitted to see at work the most effective force that has ever brought the lever to play with gentle but resistless pressure against the groaning weight of some of the worst evils done under the sun.

Strong but gentle Pressure.

Grant to us the fulcrum of a steady conviction that all men are full 'brothers in the flesh,' as Paul here embraces the slave Onesimus with his master Philemon and with himself—'no longer as a bondman, but above a bondman, a *brother beloved*, especially to me, but how much more unto thee, *in the flesh*': apply to that fulcrum the lever of the spiritual brotherhood or Christian fellowship of rights and liberties, 'a brother beloved,' not merely 'in the flesh,' but *in the Lord*'; and then place on that lever the gentle but determined hand of Christian sympathy and fellow-feeling—'if thou countest me therefore a partner, receive him as myself,'—what a

148

Paul Pleading the Subject

mass of human wrongs must begin at once to yield **Philemon** 16. to the touch, and at last give way entirely before it!

Such sentiments applied as we find them here have availed to achieve many wonders, and are destined to achieve many more, in 'raising that which is fallen down,' in easing the woes and sad lot of the oppressed, and in accomplishing many a happy revolution in social arrangements, all the more precious because accomplished without violence, bloodshed, or fraud.

To realise the power of these principles, we have **Paul himself a wonderful Illustration.** only to think of the marvellous changes they had wrought in the apostle himself. Born and bred, as he was, a very Jew of the Jews, his pride of race had succumbed before the over-mastering power of the conception that all men are full brothers according to the flesh ; and his bigotry of religion had yielded to his gospel commission to call on all men everywhere to become brothers together in the Lord.

The world had heard the sentiment before, 'I am a man, and I regard nothing with indifference which affects any fellow-man'; but in one like the apostle it ceased to be a mere sentiment, and was translated into visible fact.

Overleaping the barriers of nationality, he delighted to own himself 'the apostle of the Gentiles.' He recognises in the Phrygian Onesimus a brother in need, and proceeds to deal with the bondman as a very brother indeed. For to the once haughty Pharisee, that would have disdained to sit at meat with any other than a co-religionist, there is now, for Christ's sake, 'neither circumcised nor uncircum-

149

The Epistle of St Paul to Philemon

cised, Jew nor Greek, Barbarian nor Scythian, bond nor free.' The converted slave is nothing less to him than a 'brother in the Lord.' He has not scorned to instruct the heathen servant in the 'mysteries of the kingdom'; and he will not shrink from saying to the servant's master, You must 'receive him as myself.'

Power of Gospel Conviction. These are the triumphs in the apostle's own soul of the wonder-working alchemy of the gospel of Christ. Do not they enable us to forecast the transforming results of its influence on the laws and forces of social life? Before the vigorous operations of such convictions as these, what forms of slavery can possibly stand? or what reasons avail for their continuance and support?

Before such expressions as these: 'No longer receive him as a slave, but a brother beloved,' the bulwarks of every unnatural and oppressive system begin to totter to their base, like the walls of Jericho before the first blast of the trumpets that presaged their fall.

Onesimus is not to be received or looked on any more merely 'as a slave,' but 'above a slave.' We need not give these words greater force than their narrowest possible meaning requires, in order to appreciate their vast significance.

Each Man a Brother We are not to give them a 'licentious interpretation,' as if they implied that Onesimus was not to be held, in any sense, in bondage longer—for the apostle does not say 'not now a slave,' but simply 'not now *as* a slave.' He does not interfere with the civil relationship, but with the moral and spiritual aspect of it. Paul does not abrogate the master's

150

Paul Pleading the Subject

authority ; but by reminding him that Onesimus is first of all a brother, he tells him that he must keep this chiefly in view in dealing henceforward with his servant. The brotherhood idea must rule.

This was probably a new light to Philemon ; but it was involved in the fundamental relationship of Christ to men. Through His incarnation and His work of redemption in human nature, the lost sense of the unity of the race of mankind was being restored. The gospel revealed that original oneness, and brought into living action the consciousness of a common humanity as well as the new-born conviction of the dignity of the nature itself and the preciousness of each individual soul.

These lofty and sacred thoughts were to guide the master in all his intercourse with the slave, constituting the point of view from which he must habitually regard him. Always and by nature he had been a 'brother in the flesh,' but, in a yet higher and holier sense, the bondman had become Philemon's co-equal and fellow, a 'brother in the Lord.' Philemon must now recognise this, and act in accordance with it. There is, of course, a difference between *brother-love* and *brotherly-love*, as there is a difference between the same thing viewed *objectively* and *subjectively*. Brother-love is the disposition to own and acknowledge as a brother every one who is really a brother, while *brotherly-love* is the disposition to act the brotherly part toward any one so owned and acknowledged. We may fail in the one case and not in the other. We may fail to call and recognise as a brother one who truly is such, while brotherly enough

151

The Epistle of St Paul to Philemon

to those we acknowledge to be brothers. The one
we ought to do but not leave the other undone.

Not that Onesimus was hereby freed from service,
or entitled to despise his master's authority, and
assume a haughty, defiant, or indifferent air. Nay:
if he were no longer 'as a slave,' but 'above a
slave,' because he was a 'brother,' his service must
no longer be slavish, but brotherly : not of dread and
drudgery, but of good-will and cheerfulness.

On the other hand, in proportion as a 'brother' is
better than a 'bondman,' it would be incumbent on
Philemon to temper his requirements and tone of
command by an habitual regard to the higher and
tenderer relationship.

How can any man, consistently, maltreat or make
merchandise of another who stands doubly in a
brotherly connection with himself—a partaker at
once of the same nature, with its inalienable rights,
and of the same filial standing before God, with its
inviolable privileges ? For a sincere recognition of
the brotherly relationship must always be accompanied
by brotherly love.

**Brotherhood
Idea must
Rule.** Onesimus should be received as a 'brother
beloved.' He was so specially to the apostle, as
being his convert to the faith, and a willing helper
of him in his bonds, though a stranger to him before :
but to how much greater extent should he be owned
thus by Philemon, who knew him as his domestic,
and was now to have proof of his brotherly service
and regard !

'No distance breaks the tie of love ;
Brothers are brothers evermore ;

152

Paul Enforcing the Subject

> Nor wrong nor wrath of deadliest mood
> That magic may o'erpower.'

And the apostle, earnestly considering how he might best bring home this privilege of brotherly love to the heart and conscience of the master, proceeds now to lift the whole question into the region of that holy 'fellowship of the saints,' where all earthly distinctions are seen to melt into thin air, and reach a point where they become ready to vanish entirely away.

VI

PAUL ENFORCING THE SUBJECT

PHILEMON verse 17.

IF thou countest me therefore a partner, receive him as myself.

THE word rendered 'partner' or fellow is a very noteworthy one in connection with primitive Church life, and bears a technical Christian application here. It may be mentioned as a singular coincidence that a Greek writer of the name of Philemon (who flourished more than three centuries before this, and of whose works only fragments are extant) wrote a play with this very word for a title : *The Fellow.* The term was used both in a vulgar and in a dignified sense, like its counterpart still in our own tongue. We say, 'the man that is my *fellow*,' or, 'the *fellow* of a college'; but also with a base reference, as in Pope's line :—

'Worth makes the man, the want of it the *fellow*.'

The Epistle of St Paul to Philemon

Had the apostle said (as some have thought) to
Philemon, 'You and I are knit together in the
bonds of cordial fellowship and friendship : now
Onesimus has become one of my friends also : I
beseech you therefore, by all that is sincere and
cordial in that friendship, or as you would avoid
a rupture of it or coolness in it, do receive him as
your friend too,' he would have said much, and to
the purpose also.

This would have been the language of a warm-
hearted man ; and had a heathen philosopher gone
to that extent on behalf of a slave, he would have
exhibited no ordinary degree of humanity and social
virtue.

All this is said by the apostle, but oh ! how much
more than this he says, and how much more telling
his appeal! For the reference is not to the rights
and reciprocities of a common friendship, however
warm and true, nor to the ties of any earth-born
relationship, however close and sacred : the appeal is
made to a group of peculiarly spiritual and religious
associations and obligations, with which Philemon's
mind was more or less familiar.

The
Christian
Fellowship.
This word 'partner,' or fellow, gathered round
itself a set of the most potent, yet most tender,
sanctions that could move and sway a Christian
heart. For let us remember that as soon as the
Church of the first days is heard of, as soon as
it sprang into a visible organisation under Pentecostal influences, each member recognised in every
other member of the new community a true and real
partner in Christ Jesus and in one another.

Paul Enforcing the Subject

This sacred bond, this truly 'holy alliance,' this Philemon 17. association in the Lord, was signalised by the name of the copartnery, communion, or fellowship—a word A Sacred Bond. that plays so prominent a part in apostolic phraseology (occurring much more frequently than our common English version indicates, owing to different words being used in rendering its meaning).

'They continued stedfastly in the apostles' doctrine and *the fellowship*,' 'God is faithful, by Acts ii. 42. whom ye were called unto *the fellowship* of His Son Jesus Christ our Lord.' '*The fellowship* of 1 Cor. i. 9. the ministering to the saints.' 'The right hands of 2 Cor viii. 4. *fellowship*.' '*Fellowship* in the gospel.' 'That Gal. ii. 9. ye also may have *fellowship* with us : and truly Phil. i. 5. our *fellowship* is with the Father, and with His Son Jesus Christ. . . . If we say that we have *fellowship* with Him : . . . but if we walk in the light, as He is in the light, we have *fellowship* one with another.' 1 John i. 3, 6, 7.

What then is this fellowship, to which these and many other passages so continually bear witness ? It has a double aspect : one Godward, Christward, heavenward : the other manward, brotherward, earthward.

It was first participation (fellowship) in the Divine 2 Peter i. 4. nature, 'fellowship with the Father in the Son,' as well as the communion (or fellowship) of the Holy 2 Cor. xiii. Ghost ; the fellowship of the body and blood of the 14. Lord, the fellowship of His sufferings, of His life, of 1 Cor. x. 16. His glory — the fellowship, in short, of Christ Himself.

Out of this sprang the other grand aspect of the

The Epistle of St Paul to Philemon

Christian fellowship—a true and profound fellowship with one another.

Divine side of 'Fellowship.' Fellowship in a common sense of the Divine redeeming love, was the master principle of all those manifestations of mutual fellowship that characterised primitive Church life. For in the Son of God there had been presented not only a new revelation, but a living *embodiment* of the Divine nature. Fellowship with Christ was, therefore, participation in the fulness of the Godhead dwelling bodily in Him. The aching void in man's nature was filled, and its arid wastes were refreshed with the downpour of heaven's mercy.

And just as when after the summer's drought a spirit of languishing is on the face of the earth, if the windows of heaven be opened, and the rains descend in full flood, the deep springs among the hills, that were cut off before, begin to burst up again from their secret sources, so when once a new sense of Divine grace and fellowship descends upon our nature, and the cross of Christ reveals the breaking of clouds of blessing from on high, the well-springs of men's hearts are reached, the fountains of the great deep are broken up, and there begins to gush forth the tide of a new life in such exhaustless streams of 'peace on earth and goodwill toward men' as to make the 'wilderness and solitary place to be glad for them, and the desert to rejoice and blossom as the rose.'

Hence those revelations of ardent zeal and the glowing fervours of cordiality which lent such attractiveness to the holy Christian communion.

Paul Enforcing the Subject

This holy and happy fellowship, so full of warm Philemon attachments and mutual helpfulness, and so different 17. from the wrangling tone of embittered and embitter- Human side ing religious parties, or the din of philosophic sects, of Fellow-
ship. had its root in the felt sense of a sacred copartnery with Christ the Lord.

There was thus an 'enthusiasm of *humanity*' fed and sustained by a corresponding 'enthusiasm of *Divinity.*' Nothing was too high, nothing too arduous for the spirit that thrilled through the exalted experiences of such a fellowship. To persuade men everywhere to become the present happy, enriched, and free shareholders in its saving benefits —to see themselves heirs of God by being joint-heirs with Christ—nothing less and nothing else was contemplated by those who already enjoyed the exhaustless boon.

Caught up into the absorbing consciousness of this Fellowship Divine copartnership, the converts presented to the at Work. eyes of an astonished world the spectacle of one body and one spirit, swept along in the full current of the 'one Lord, one faith, one baptism : one God and Father of all,' who was evidently not only above them all, but 'in and through them all,' moving them on in the same one united 'hope of their calling.'

We read of the early converts that they were all 'of one heart and of one mind.' They met 'with one accord in one place.' Their fellow-Christians were 'the brethren'; and their organisation was 'the fellowship,' while, in the self-abandonment of a Christian devotedness, they could afford to be ecclesiastical communists for Christ's sake with great

The Epistle of St Paul to Philemon

Philemon
17. central and common funds and yet without either violating the rights of property, or doing damage to any moral or social claims.

This was what acted like a spell upon men's minds, and led multitudes to whisper, with solemn wonderment: 'Behold how these Christians love one another.' The vision of this holy, happy, and tender fellowship was like the dawn of a new era upon earth: the omen of returning calm to many a doubt-tossed spirit: a light from heaven to many wistful gazers in the dark, whose yearning question, 'Watchman, what of the night?' was now receiving its Isaiah xxi. 11, 12. hopeful answer: 'The night cometh: and *also the day*: if ye will inquire, inquire ye: return: come.'

The genial glow of such a fellowship was the sunny spot, the warm hearth, that drew around it the sin-smitten, shivering outcasts of humanity.

A ' levelling-up' Spirit. And what a bond of union it became to those who felt its charm! What an 'esprit de corps' it developed! What a 'levelling-up' process it inaugurated in Christian social life, and what a potent influence it exerted in kindling the sparks of generous love into a blaze of sympathetic attachment and mutual service!

Paul appeals to Fellow-ship. To this high and holy fellowship the apostle now makes his appeal. It is the best arrow in his quiver, and he reserves it to the last. How deftly he dismisses it from his bow and sends it straight to the mark!

By all the sanctities of the noblest fellowship man can know with man or hold with the Lord, Paul now conjures Philemon. By all its common rights and privileges, by all its blessed associations and eternally

Paul Enforcing the Subject

Philemon 17. enduring bonds, by all its kindly ties and welcome experiences, he hopes he will prove loyal to its principles and claims.

It is for the honour of this fellowship in Christ the apostle is now concerned. Within that hallowed enclosure the richest master is the Lord's servant, and the meanest slave is nothing else. Here the greatest are those that serve : the humblest are the highest.

The present question falls within the sweep of this common Christian fellowship. For Philemon to refuse its rights and privileges to Onesimus would look like a breach of Christian communion with the apostle himself. 'I and Onesimus are one in the Lord : he is a fellow-communicant with me in Christ, and I with him.'

Is Philemon to despise or disown this relationship ? Give Fellow-ship free play. It would be like a threatened rupture of their communion bond ; and might prove a deadly wound to their personal Christian intimacy. Surely Philemon will never think to run such risks. 'If then thou count me a partner, regard Onesimus, if not in all respects, yet in this one respect, as myself, your fellow Christian ; for he is a fellow Christian of mine. Will you receive him and treat him as such ? letting the spirit of our common fellowship give tone and colour to all your intercourse with him in daily life. For as members of the same body we must suffer or rejoice together : as partners of the like precious faith our interests are one.

'If therefore' (or rather, as the apostle is not making a supposition, but expressing a conclusion,

159

The Epistle of St Paul to Philemon

since therefore) 'thou countest me a fellow-Christian, receive him like one, and extend to him, as you would to me, a happy and cheerful welcome, a cordial and affectionate embrace, an earnest grasp of the right hand of fellowship, in the name of the Lord.'

VII

PAUL GUARDING THE SUBJECT

PHILEMON verses 18-20.

BUT if he wronged thee in any respect, or oweth aught, put that to mine account ; I, Paul, have written it with mine own hand, I will repay : so that I may not say to thee that thou owest to me even thine own self besides. Yea, brother, may I have joy of thee in the Lord : refresh my heart in Christ.

WE might be apt to think that the 'community of goods,' which was at work in the fellowship of the primitive Church, must have operated against the rights of private property. A little reflection, however, on the matter will convince us that its effect was to add to the safeguards (by enhancing the sense of responsibility) of personal ownership.

It stands quite distinguished from all schemes of mere socialistic or political 'communism'—in method, in motive, in object, and in result.

In *method.*—They have usually had recourse to measures of legal coercion, if not of physical violence ; it relied on pure and simple voluntariness—on spontaneity from within, not on pressure from without. Peter said to Ananias : 'While your possession remained, was it not thine own ? and after it was sold, was it not in thine own power ? '

160

Paul Guarding the Subject

In *motive.*—Its co-operative temper of mutual **Philemon 18-20.** **Pious.** interest and goodwill sprang not merely from the self-denying virtues, but from a sense of immeasurable indebtedness to the Lord, for whom they were merely stewards of all they possessed. 'No man reckoned ought that he had his own.' It was lent him on trust ; and this being the peculiar tenure by which he enjoyed his worldly substance, he felt himself answerable to the Lord for the way he laid it out. This was the unique motive.

In *object.*—Earthly communisms have sought their **Unworldly and for Christian Objects.** paradise mainly in a redistribution of wealth on more equal terms—often creating an atmosphere of delusive hopes, too ethereal for anything but monomania to breathe, and, by a series of chimerical arrangements and appliances, conjuring up mighty air-castles, at whose fading shapes the irony of bitter experience has had to point its mocking finger. Its object was to ameliorate the evils of human condition by rectifying the evils of human nature.

In *result.*—How many communistic experiments **Gracious and Beneficent.** have run their course through disorder, robbery, and insurrection, till quenched at last in the horrors of fire and bloodshed—a scene of indiscriminate ruin and misery, with its legacies of bitterness, envy, and ill-will. But the spirit and principles that regulated the workings of Christian communion created the tenderest consideration for one another's rights, and the deepest feelings of sanctity for one another's possessions.

We have an exemplary illustration of this in the present verses. What an example Paul affords

L   161

The Epistle of St Paul to Philemon

'to provide things honest in the sight of all men!'

The Christian fellowship may forgive and overlook much in the spirit of that charity which covers a multitude of sins; but it can never relax the bonds of moral obligation, nor connive at violations of right and duty. Whatever view we take of the offence of Onesimus (and we are not lightly to assume him guilty of robbery or embezzlement), there were two things in it that had to be dealt with.

Presuming that there was no depth of guilt beyond his clandestine escape, there was a wrong done to Philemon (in the shape of an affront to his honour, or a slur cast on his character as a master, which needed to be punished or pardoned), and there was damage or loss entailed by the bondman's absence from service, which needed to be refunded or repaired.

To the former the apostle has already attended by asking Philemon to overlook the fault of Onesimus, and receive him kindly for his sake; but the master might still say: 'I forgive him heartily, as a Christian, the offence he has committed against me, but what of the question of my loss? Are my bondmen to be encouraged to leave me, and when they come back penitent, and ask forgiveness, is it simply to be granted, and no more said? And am I to be left helpless and without redress? This would be ruinous —a premium on disobedience and flight!'

The apostle now takes note of this aspect of the case, and provides the remedy. Philemon's just claims must be respected. His rights must be

162

regarded. He must be guaranteed and indemnified **Philemon** against loss. **18-20.**

'But if he wronged thee in any respect, or oweth aught'—that is, in so far as by his misdoing towards thee he may be in your debt—full reparation is your due. And as accounts cannot be settled by expressions of regret, however sincere, or by promises that other debts shall not be incurred in the future, as, in short, the only way to meet debts is to pay them, and Onesimus is himself unable to satisfy your loss, will you allow me to become his surety for the amount, that I may not seem to trifle with your private affairs? I will repay thee. Witness my name, PAUL, in mine own handwriting.

Perhaps the apostle wrote the whole letter with his own hand—we are, at least, not precluded from supposing so; but this was an unusual thing for him to do with his fettered wrist; and if he did it in this case, it would be a special token of friendship for Philemon.

The chief point to note is the business-like style **In Business** in which he settles a business transaction. In what **Fashion.** a practical, common-sense way he deals with the subject! As 'an oath for confirmation is an end of all strife,' so a document properly endorsed is a safeguard against all mere 'understandings,' which are so apt to turn out 'misunderstandings' in the end. A good man's word is as sure as his bond; but where satisfaction has to be rendered to others, especially where there is variance among them, the most delicate sense of honour will never think it derogatory to itself to afford a properly-attested voucher.

The Epistle of St Paul to Philemon

Oh, what mischief in families, in friendships, in Churches, would be avoided by attention like the apostle's to simple safeguards against dissension and dissatisfaction!

A Question of Surety-ship.
From this friendly example of Paul we may see how lawful it is for one to become surety for another, and how Christian a thing it is to engage, within the limits of our own ready resources, in aiding the pecuniary difficulties of those we can truly serve: though it behoves all to mark carefully how Paul acts in this matter, as 'a man of affairs,' on sound moral and business principles, if they would not be foolishly entangled in the meshes of a rash or useless suretyship.

And what a light is shed on the gospel idea of making reparation to God by means of a substitute, according to this earthly analogy! How finely the apostle here follows in the footsteps of Him who, on a higher plane, offered Himself as pledge or pawn for us who had failed to render the service that was due!

A Gospel Analogy.
Sin is no doubt much more than debt, but it is debt in so far as human defalcations stand in the account with God. Through melancholy faithlessness and dereliction and apostasy toward Him, what debts have been accumulating beyond all human power to liquidate!

Neither regrets nor promises can here avail. Debts must be paid, if they would creditably be written off. The grace of the Lord Jesus admits of Him being debited. To the trusting soul He says: 'I am your written and covenant surety'; and so far as sin is a load of debt to God, it is His alone to say: 'Put this down to My account. I will repay.'

Paul Guarding the Subject

Not as if there were any transference of moral Philemon qualities, or confusion of merit. Human guilt or 18-20. blameworthiness can never be transferred to Christ, How Christ is our only imputed or reckoned to His account. What is Surety. actually transferred is the liability. And so must Christ's merit be ever His own—its benefits only can be transferred, when it itself is imputed or put to any human account.

In this sense Christ is ever holding Himself forth as able and ready to bear away the burden of human debt, and cancel sin, in the account of any soul with God.

When the apostle adds, 'I may not say to thee A Matter that thou owest to me even thine own self besides,' Personal to Philemon. we should utterly mistake his meaning were we to regard him as if desirous of evading the full force of his promise just given, or as if he were half retracting it. No : should Philemon require its fulfilment, Paul holds himself bound to render it without demur ; should Philemon, on the other hand, waive his claim, Paul cannot himself make such.a proposal, though he desires to leave Philemon free to offer it.

If Philemon should feel that it would hardly do for him to hold by Paul's bond and exact the payment, the apostle delicately and almost playfully indicates how easily he may be released. 'Accept my pledge, that I may not have to suggest how much more you are in my debt than this liability I have now assumed : owing me, as you do, your own self (your better and higher self), besides what you now in addition owe me for Onesimus ?

There can be no worse prostituting of things

The Epistle of St Paul to Philemon

sacred than to make a handle of them for personal
or worldly profit. But such a thought is far enough
from the apostle's mind. He is simply concerned
for the honour and credit of Philemon, and is keenly
solicitous that he should come nobly, and with an
enhanced Christian reputation, out of the present
ordeal.

Is it nothing to the apostle whether Philemon be
magnanimous or not? Is it nothing to Paul whether
Philemon stamp the present opportunity with a befitting impress, or act in such a way as shall bear
the happiest reflection afterwards in his own mind,
and win the highest approval from one to whom,
under God, Philemon owed so much?

'Yes, brother,' he adds, with great tenderness of
regard and affection, 'I know you will let me enjoy
some good, like yourself, from all this'; and then,
playfully reverting to the meaning of Onesimus:
'Seeing you are getting service from me now, you
will not refuse to render me, in the Lord, a little
recompense of service in return. Thou, who dost
refresh the hearts of saints, wilt never allow my
heart to languish: thou wilt not make mine an
exception! Let me have comfort and good cheer in
Christ!' Not that I doubt your readiness for a
moment to let me enjoy with yourself some special
Christian comfort, some special satisfaction in the
Lord, but I am solicitous about such a happy outcome and issue of all this kind providence to you.

VIII

PAUL COMMENDING THE SUBJECT

PHILEMON, verses 21, 22.

HAVING confidence in thy obedience I have written to thee, knowing that thou wilt also do more than I say. But at the same time be preparing also a lodging for me : for I am hoping that through your prayers I shall be given unto you.

THE apostle, in beginning to draw the letter to a **Philemon** close, pauses for a moment to glance back at the **21, 22.** spirit in which he has written it.

He has had thorough confidence in Philemon's **Paul's** sincere desire to know and do whatever is Christianly **Confidence in Philemon.** good and right.

What a token of this confidence he had given at the outset, in that he says, ' I will not enjoin thee as an apostle, but will rather entreat thee as a friend and brother.' What a still further token of confidence that Paul sends back Onesimus, and entrusts his interests wholly and unreservedly in the hands of his master, without any previous bargaining or binding him down first to receive and treat the fugitive kindly ! No : he trusts him. He has confidence in his Christian character and disposition.

But perhaps the highest proof of his confidence is to be found in the present verse, where Paul expresses his assurance that Philemon will so interpret and enter into the spirit of his pleadings as not to be restrained within the mere letter of his instructions.

It may seem, perhaps, to militate against the **A Proof of** completeness of Paul's trust that he introduces **it.** the word ' obedience.' ' Having confidence in thy

The Epistle of St Paul to Philemon

obedience.' But we are not to think of this as obedience to the apostle's own authority—though he might have put it on that ground—for the reference is to the principle of obedience at large. 'Having confidence in your obeying (not my authority, which I have waived, but) all that you conceive the Lord Himself requires of you, all that the gospel, so far as you know it, demands, all that your conscience dictates—in this spirit I have been writing you.'

Paul would not have any blind submission to himself from Philemon, but intelligent conviction. To this end he has been putting before him arguments, statements and wishes, that might serve as persuasives to a certain line of action, without saying where he was to stop short.

The beauty and largeness of Paul's confidence lay in his not having treated Philemon as a mere babe in Christ, who needed to be ordered about and commanded in every detail, but as one who could be trusted to apply principles for himself, and carry them out in the way that his own enlightened convictions suggested, under a felt sense of personal responsibility to the Lord.

A Well-Grounded Confidence. The apostle has very good reason for thinking so. His is not a blind confidence in Philemon. It rests upon evidence which he has mentioned in the opening of the letter. He knows of Philemon's high Christian character and attainments: and he has all along proceeded on this basis. He has appealed on behalf of Onesimus, not to any particular precepts, but to Christian principles.

Paul Commending the Subject

The value and importance of these he has been
insisting upon, and been anxious that Philemon
should realise their bearing on the case of Onesimus;
but he has not applied them as if judging for him.
To commend them he has left no stone unturned :
omitted no plea that could legitimately be adduced :
kept back nothing of his persuasive power : taken
advantage of every favourable consideration, and, at
every opening that offered, has poured in some telling
fact, allusion, or motive.   The following is a characteristic passage—one of those curiously long-drawn
elaborations to which the old authors occasionally
devote their strength :—

'Every word in this Epistle almost hath the force
of a motive : and seasoning his cause with wisdom
and his doings with art, Paul so creepeth into
Philemon's bosom, and closeth with him at a
sudden, that by no means he can start from him.
Sometimes by loving titles ; sometimes by artificial
insinuations ; sometimes by favourable preventing of
objections ; sometimes by rhetorical persuasions ;
sometimes by earnest preparations ; sometimes by
charitable mitigations ; sometimes by strong obligations ; sometimes by deep protestations ; sometimes
by fit revocations ; and sometimes by forcible arguments—as it were by so many courteous *congés* and
vehement adjurations he dealeth with and prevaileth
in such sort with him, as Popilius, the Roman
Ambassador, against Antiochus, King of Syria, who,
having delivered his message from the Senate, made
a circle about him with his rod, and charged him to
put off all delays and give him present answer before

The Epistle of St Paul to Philemon

Philemon
21, 22.

Attersoll's
(*Philemon*)
Dedication,
A.D. 1612.

he departed out of it. Thus doth the apostle lay
his net and cast his chain about Philemon, that he
hampereth him fast and holdeth him close before he
is aware of any such matter.' The apostle, however,
does not affect to dictate the precise ways of carrying his pleadings into effect.

**Something
left to
Philemon's
Intelligence.** His design is to secure that Philemon receive
Onesimus as a brother, both by nature and by grace,
even as he would receive Paul himself into his
religious fellowship in the Church; but how this
is to be done, and by what special acts it is to
be manifested, Paul does not mention. He hints
at much, but literally specifies nothing, and con-
descends on no particulars. 'I have been writing
you in all trustfulness, for I know you will do more
than I have allowed myself to express in words.'

**Does Paul
hint at
Manu-
mission?** What is this something more at which he points?
Is it the manumission of Onesimus? Some have
been disposed to doubt if the subject of the bondman's emancipation be here hinted at, even faintly.
It will, however, be hard to convince any one familiar
with the apostle's arguments and pleas, that the
thought was not before the writer's mind.

Paul has asked everything short of that—he has
used arguments that cover it and strongly suggest it,
and anything more than he has said seems to require
it. If in all this, however, there is no allusion to
Onesimus having his liberty, it must be because
there is room for so much more, and that manumission is only one of many possible results which
Paul contemplates.

We conceive the apostle purposely refrains from

being more specific, so as to admit of Philemon **Philemon** putting the largest construction on the marks of **21, 22.** brotherhood and goodwill to be conferred upon Onesimus. As if he should say: ' I have thorough confidence that you will not only not disappoint my reasonable expectations, but that, with the feeling that I might have asked more, you will not shrink from giving practical effect to the principles I have laid down, so far as you understand them. I am so persuaded of this that I desire to give you in conclusion another pledge of my entire confidence. I am coming to see you, and I know I shall find no occasion to feel aggrieved about this matter when I come.'

Such is the connection we conceive between verse 21 and verse 22. To shut up all, the apostle intimates to Philemon a design which, though it might seem foreign to the main business, yet might tend as much as anything that may be said to promote it. ' But withal prepare me a lodging also.' It is a known observation that letters do not blush. What men would be ashamed to ask in person, that they are bold enough to ask by letter : and it is as true that the readers of letters do not blush ; they are hardy enough to deny that to their absent friends which they could not refuse them if present. The apostle therefore intimates his inten- **Smalridge,** tion shortly to visit Philemon at Colossæ. The *Sermon* **xxxix.** commission to prepare a lodging can hardly be regarded than as meant to bear indirectly in favour of Onesimus ; and if any think not, we can simply say it is the only verse out of the twenty-five that

The Epistle of St Paul to Philemon

Philemon 21, 22. has no look in that direction, and that whatever was the purpose of the apostle, there can hardly be any doubt as to the effect on Philemon, in quickening him to a hearty compliance with what he, at least, understood to be conveyed by the letter.

One direct and cordial Request. We should, however, utterly misconceive if we associated the coarse idea of 'espionage,' or 'pressure,' being brought to bear on Philemon in connection with the visit. All that seems to be meant is: 'Having a probable opportunity of seeing you soon, I will readily advise with you further on the matter; none the less trusting, however, that before I come you may have promptly and satisfactorily settled it all.'

The confidential tone of the announcement must have been highly reassuring to Philemon, while the cordial tone of the request must have been truly gratifying.

'Withal prepare me also a lodging.' He does not say where—the expression being merely a familiar desire for Philemon's friendly offices in securing accommodation for him anywhere, though doubtless it would result in his being welcome as an honoured guest under Philemon's own hospitable roof. 'For I am hoping that through your prayers I shall be given unto you.'

A last tender touch. Who can resist the pathos of such a tender turn? It could not but lend new fervency to these prayers, and send a thrill of holy and thankful joy through all 'the Church in the house.'

To this the apostle seems to summon them by the very word he uses for his release; an act, as he

172

Paul Commending the Subject

would have them consider it, not so much of human **Philemon**
clemency as of Divine mercy, both to him and to ^{21, 22.}
them, attributable, under God, to the efficacy of
their prayers on his behalf.

It is interesting to find that good and devout Dr
Doddridge preached from his text : 'I trust that
through your prayers I shall be given (back) unto
you,' on occasion of his being restored to health,
after a most dangerous attack of fever. With his
usual unction and affectionate simplicity, he applies
Paul's case to his own, attributing his recovery to
his people's prayers, and especially to those of some
young members of his flock, who had continued much
in prayer for him on the night which proved the
favourable turning-point in the crisis.

CONCLUSION

PARTING SALUTATIONS AND BENEDICTION

PHILEMON, verses 23-25.

THERE saluteth thee Epaphras, my fellow-prisoner in Christ Jesus, Mark, Aristarchus, Demas, Luke, my fellow-labourers. The grace of our Lord Jesus Christ be with your spirit. [Amen.]

Philemon 23-25. Greetings from Friends. THE letter concludes as usual with greetings and benediction—the salutations from friends being addressed to Philemon personally, while the benediction is extended (as the change to the plural in it shows) to all the others as well who are named at the beginning of the letter.

In thus associating the brethren who are with him, he would hint that they concur in the sentiments and object of the letter, while by such courtesies he would exemplify the spirit of kindly interest and regard which Christian friends should exhibit and cultivate toward one another.

The salutations are naturally from the same persons who join in the greetings to the Colossian Church (Coloss. iv. 10-14), both epistles being written about the same time—the only difference being the omission here of Jesus Justus, probably because he was not present when this letter was written, though he was before the General Church Epistle to Colossæ was finished.

174

Salutations and Benediction

The order of the names is substantially the same, **Philemon** save that Epaphras holds here the place of honour, **23-25.** being mentioned first, as Aristarchus is in the Epistle **Epaphras.** to the Church of Colossæ. The reason for the transposition seems to lie in the peculiar title 'fellow-prisoner,' which is given here to Epaphras, there to Aristarchus.

It would appear as if the brethren took turns in voluntarily sharing the apostle's imprisonment, so as to minister to him in his bonds, 'not being ashamed of his chain.' By such a 'fellowship of sufferings'—a much-coveted honour, no doubt— how much they must have refreshed his heart!

But besides this, we should observe regarding Epaphras that in Colossians he is honoured with the special designation 'bondman of Christ Jesus,' which the apostle nowhere uses but of himself, except once of Timothy (Philip. i. 1), and which apparently indicates some very peculiar service and suffering for the gospel.

'Epaphras' is to be regarded as a shortened or provincial form of the common name Epaphroditus, though we are not to confound the two companions of Paul's Roman captivity, the Philippian Epaph-roditus and the Colossian Epaphras.

We can readily understand the prominence given **One of your-** both here and in Colossians to Epaphras, for he was **selves, Col.** **iv. 12.** a Colossian, and indeed one of the chief, if not the **Coloss.** very first, of the bearers of the gospel to that city. **i. 7.**

The other four who send greetings are classed together as 'fellow-labourers': Mark and Aristarchus **Col. iv. 11.** belonging to the circumcision, while Demas and

175

The Epistle of St Paul to Philemon

Philemon 23-25. Luke were Gentile Christians—an interesting group, having fuller, and in some respects more peculiar, associations to us than to Philemon, each name representing some special vicissitude in Paul's experience of the changes of life.

Mark. If, as seems certain, the Mark here introduced is the John Mark of the earlier times, he may represent the misunderstandings that embitter life, but happily also the cementing of broken friendships and the healing of old wounds.

The occasion, as he was, of sharp contention and **Acts xv. 38, 39.** of angry alienation for a time between himself, Barnabas, and Paul, how pleasing to find him among the associates of the apostle, and ere long to be **2 Tim. iv. 11.** specially signalised as 'profitable for the ministry' to the apostle in his last and severest imprisonment.

Aristarchus. Aristarchus stands associated with a different **Acts xix. 29.** kind of crisis in the apostle's career. His name is linked to a scene of turmoil and danger. Along with Gaius, he had been thrust into the deadly breach between the infuriated Ephesian mob and 'this Paul,' whom it sought as a victim.

With all the spirit and courage of the Macedonian that he was, he would not have shrunk, as one of 'Paul's companions in travel,' from giving his life 'in *his* life's stead.' Aristarchus would be to the apostle a symbol and memorial of a happy deliverance in a dark hour of peril.

Demas. But what shall we say of Demas, a memorable **2 Tim. iv. 10.** and melancholy illustration, as he was soon to become, of the disappointments of life, with its treacheries and false-play? 'Demas hath forsaken

176

Salutations and Benediction

me, having loved this present world.' This was **Philemon**
the Judas in Paul's fellowship circle, a deserter from **23-25.**
him in a time of deepest need, if not also from
Christ, for the world's sake.

> 'The martyr's cell no safety lends,
> To him who wants the martyr's heart.'

The last name, that of Luke, the chronicler and **Luke.**
sharer of Paul's journeys, will ever remain associated
in a special way with Paul's bodily health, 'the
beloved physician' having attached himself to the
apostle as a friendly medical adviser—the first in
that long illustrious line who have wedded the
healing art to the triumphs of the gospel.

If then Epaphras stand for a reminder of the
great 'fellowship of suffering,' may not Mark speak
of life's strife, with its separations and reunions;
Aristarchus of its hazards and anxieties; Demas of
its inner disappointments and sorrows; and Luke
(if only by way of contrast) of its outer ailments
and frailties?

But alongside of all these experiences, to transform
and sweeten them, stands the ever-ready 'grace of
the Lord Jesus,' like the tree of healing of old to be
cast into the waters of Marah, that they be no longer
bitter.

With a prayer for this grace Paul had opened **All-compre-hensive Wish.**
the epistle, and with a prayer for this grace he now
will close. It is the most all-inclusive wish for good
he can indite in so few words—the free and saving
favour of the Lord, with all its holy and happy
influences for soul and body, for time and for eternity.

The Epistle of St Paul to Philemon

Philemon 23-25. This grace sanctifies earth's fellowships, and protects them from degeneracy and social corruption. It raises life above the entanglements of *ennui* and chagrin, of cynicism and despair. It weans the heart from the world, without permitting it to be soured. It lends dignity to suffering, and gilds the gloom of sorrow with radiant hope.

2 Cor. xii. 9. To the apostle had been often verified the soul-sustaining words, ' My grace is sufficient for thee.'

As the day grows, the warmth increases and the shadows flee away; so, as grace is realised, the heart basks and suns itself in the glow of heaven's love, and everything gets bathed in heaven's own light.

With this grace to soothe and solace himself, Paul felt

> ' He could behold
> The strife and tumults of this troubled world
> With the strong eye that sees the promised day
> Dawn through a night of tempest. Thus his heart
> Was healed and harmonized.'

' May this grace of the Lord Jesus be with your spirit, as it is with mine.' For he says, not, ' The grace of the Lord Jesus be with you,' but, with more impassioned earnestness, ' be with your spirit.'

Num. i. 2. Jerome thus explains, ' As the children of Israel were reckoned according to their *heads* the better part of man, so while grace pervades the whole nature, Paul refers it to the higher and greater part, *the spirit*, put here by synecdoche for the *entire* man.

Nor does he say ' your spirits' (though numbers of persons are referred to), but, with a realising

178

Salutations and Benediction

sense of their inner vital unity and community with **Philemon** one another in Christ Jesus, whereby their hearts **23-25.** should meet and flow together in holy concord, he takes the higher nature, where grace reigns and which is the seat of a common Christian consciousness, and so bids them farewell in one emphatic word : 'The grace of the Lord Jesus be with your *spirit.*'

APPENDIX

ON THE BIBLIOGRAPHY OR LITERATURE OF THE EPISTLE TO PHILEMON

PATRISTIC (GREEK).—*Chrysostom* (A.D. 348-407), three Homilies, very vigorous and eloquent, as usual, with preface, translated, in Oxford *Library of the Fathers* ; his fellow-student at Antioch, *Theodore* (of Mopsuestia, A.D. 350-429)—consult specially 'Theodore of Mopsuestia on the minor Epistles of St Paul,' by H. B. Swete, B.D., Cambridge University Press, 1880 ; and *Theodoret* (of Cyrus, A.D. 386-459), who was also from Antioch. (*See* Abbé Migne's *Library of the Fathers*, Paris).

LATIN CONTEMPORARIES.—Jerome (A.D. 346-420), and Hilary, who belongs to the same date (surnamed for distinction *the Deacon,* whose comments are found in the works of Ambrose).

MEDIÆVAL.—These commentaries are chiefly *Catenæ*, or extracts from the earlier Fathers. Even minds like those of Bede (A.D. 673-735), and of Thomas Aquinas, five centuries later (A.D. 1225-1274), attempt nothing original in their expositions of Paul's Epistles. The three most prominent writers on Philemon are the Englishman *Alcuin* of York (A.D. 735-804): *Œcumenius*, of Tricca in Thessaly, two centuries later ; and chiefly *Theophylact*, the dis-

Appendix

tinguished Archbishop of Bulgaria, at the end of the eleventh and beginning of the twelfth century, who ranks so high among the lights of the Eastern Church. The *Annotationes* which pass under the name of Cælius Sedulius of either the *fifth* or the *eighth* century, *In Omnes S. Pauli Epistolas*, were published at Basil in 1538.

REFORMATION EPOCH. — *Lutheran Church.* — Luther's *Enarrationes Epistolarum* (1521): his associate at Wittenberg, Bugenhagen's (commonly called *Pomeranus*, 1524) *Adnotationes*, and his disciple Brenz's (Brentius, 1499-1570) *Commentaria. Reformed Churches.*—Calvin's *Commentary* 1554, the French Protestant Marloratus (1561), Beza (1565), Lambertus Danæus (Geneva, 1579), Dudley Fenner's *Interpretatio* 1586, Feuardentius (Paris, 1588), and Principal Rollock, *Analysis Logica* (Edinburgh, 1598).

SEVENTEENTH CENTURY.—The impulse of the Reformation era communicated its exegetical spirit to the greater part of the following century. This was felt even in the Romish Church, whose greatest commentators, Professor Van Steen (of Louvain), better known by his Latinised name of Cornelius a Lapide, and Van Est (Estius, of Douay)—the one a Belgian and the other Dutch—published contemporaneously, probably the two most valuable expositions on St Paul's Epistles ever produced by Romish divines (an abridged form of them both by John of Gorcum, being specially serviceable), though differing greatly in their plan from one another.

The Epistle to Philemon receives its own share of

181

Appendix

attention in the other general commentaries of the century, such as Piscator (Fischer) of Herborn 1601, the elder Crellius, the great Socinian expounder, and his co-religionist Jonas Slichtingius a Bukowiek (*Bib. Frat. Polon.*, 1656); Grotius (1641-50), The Westminster Assembly's *Annotations* (Lond. 1651), Hammond (1653), with Le Clerc's additions (1698), Matthew Poole, the English Presbyterian divine (*Synopsis*, 1669-74), and also his *Annotations* which he did not live to complete—his learned contemporary Dr Collinge being the Annotator on *Philemon* and other of the O. and N. T. Books.—Trapp, Mayer, Dickson of Glasgow (*Expos. of all St Paul's Epistles*, London, 1659), and the *Critici Sacri*, Annotations on this particular epistle, by the Jurist, Scipio Gentilis (published separately before, in 1618, and edited again in 1774 by J. H. de Ruyter, 4to, Traj. ad Rhen), Price, La Valla, Erasmus, Vatablus, Drusius, Casaubon, Abraham Scultetus, and others. The special commentaries are those of William Attersol (1612, London, valuable and rare Puritan volume of over 500 folio pages), who thus naïvely defends its *size*, in dedicating it to the Right Worshipful Sir Thomas Pelham—'Agesilaus, King of Lacedæmon, when one praised a certain orator that he could stretch out small matters at large and length and amplify them with many words, both fitly and fully answered him, 'But I cannot think him a good shoemaker that would put a great and wide shoe upon a slender foot.' There be many, I fear, who, considering the shortness of this epistle, and comparing it with the largeness of my exposition, will be

Appendix

ready to suppose and surmise that to a little city 1 have set up wide gates, and to a slender body have fashioned a wide garment. But if these partial judges weigh the cause aright . . . I doubt not but they will rather think that to a great foot I have fitted and applied a little shoe. For this epistle, though it be short in words and comprehended in little compass, . . . is a right great epistle, and as one saith in another case, *Verborum parva, sed rerum secunda,*' etc. The Baptist Dan Dyke (*A Fruitful Commentarie,* posthumous, 1618), William Jones, D.D. (1636), John Vincent (Paris, 1647), Crucius (Haarlem, 1649), Frankenstein (Leipsic and Halle, 1657), Hummelius (Tiguri, 1670), and Fechtius (*Exegetica Expos.,* Rostoch, 1696).

EIGHTEENTH CENTURY.—General Commentaries: Whitby (1703), and the great French Catholic, Calmet (1707-17), Beausobre and Lenfant (1718), Wolfius (*Curæ Philol. in N.T.,* 1725-35), the incomparable Bengel (*Gnomon,* 1742), the elder Rosenmüller (*Scholia,* 1777), and Macknight (*Apostol. Epis.,* 1795)—besides the more popular comments in Matthew Henry (the compilers who 'gathered up the fragments,' as they themselves phrase it, on Philemon, are *unknown*—see preface to Romans) and Thomas Scott, who were just within the century, the former at its beginning and the latter at its close ; while Philip Doddridge, with his *Family Expositor,* came in between them, as did also Wells (1798), Gill (1746-48), and Guyse (1747).

In 1731, George Benson issued in the form of a shilling pamphlet his *Paraph. and notes on Philemon,*

Appendix

following it up with similar others on five more Epistles—the whole being issued in a 4to vol., 1752, with valuable dissertations.

The only other separate Expositions of Philemon the whole century affords are those of Schmidt (Leipsic, 1786), and Klotzsch (Viteb. 1792).

Bishop Smalridge reviewed the Epistle with great conciseness and beauty in a single sermon (Oxford, folio, No. 39, 1724), as did also Dr Nathaniel Marshall, though less successfully (*Sermons*, 1731, vol. ii., No. 13); while the famous physiognomist Lavater, pastor of Zürich, published thirty-nine sermons on it (*Predigten über den Brief an den Philemon*, St Gallen, 1785-6, 2 vols.).

NINETEENTH CENTURY.—General Commentaries for popular use, embracing this Epistle : Dr Adam Clarke (1810-26), Barnes (1832-47), Jamieson, Fausset, and Brown (1868), and that on the New Test. for English readers, edited by Bishop Ellicot— third vol., containing Philemon, by Dr Alfred Barry, afterwards Bishop of Sydney.

New Test. Critical Commentaries : Bloomfield, Alford, Wordsworth, Webster and Wilkinson; German : De Wette, Wiesinger (Olshausen Series), and above all Meyer (translated for Messrs Clark, Edinburgh).

Grammatical and Exegetical Commentaries on this Epistle by itself, or in conjunction with others : Niemeyer (Halle, 1802), Wildshut (*Traj. ad Rhen.*, 1809), Heinrichs (1828, continuation of Koppe), Hagenbach (Basle, 1829), Storr and Flatt (Tübingen, 1829), Rothe (Bremæ, 1844), Demme (Breslau, 1844),

184

Appendix

Koch (Zürich, 1846), Peterman (Berlin, 1844), Peile (London, 1848-52), Bleek (1865), Llewelyn Davies (London, 1866), and particularly Holtzmann's essay, *Der Brief an Philemon* in the *Zeitschr. f. Weiss-Theol.* 1873, with *Betrachtungen über den Brief St Pauli an dem Philemon im Hinblick auf die Sociale Frage von Grützmacher* (Bremen, 1879). In *The Speaker's Commentary* (Canon Cook, editor, 1881), the notes on Philemon are by Bishop Wm. Alexander, now Archbishop of Armagh. In *The Cambridge Bible* the notes on Philemon are by the late Bishop Moule of Durham (1893).

Of the highest critical value are the Commentaries of Bishop Ellicott (1st ed. 1857, 3rd ed. 1865), and Dr J. B. Lightfoot, Bishop of Durham (London, 1875, and 3rd Edit. 1879)—the former more grammatically minute, and the latter more masterly in its interpreting power; while, perhaps, the most serviceable of all is that by Van Oosterzee of Utrecht (in Lange's *Bible-work*), as translated and supplemented by Horatio B. Hackett, D.D., who incorporates with it the whole of his own valuable Notes and Exposition of the Epistle (prepared for the American Bible Union, New York, 1860) in Clark's *Foreign Theological Library* (Edinburgh, 1868). The most recent critical commentary is that in T. & T. Clark's *International Series* (Edin. 1900).

Finally, we may note a few Pulpit Expositions of this Epistle: Single Discourses (going over *the whole of it*—there are many others on individual verses)— J. S. Buckminster (the eloquent American Unitarian of Boston, died 1812, at the age of 28); Thomas Parry (Archdeacon and subsequently Bishop of

Appendix

Barbadoes, preached in Antigua, 12mo, London, 1834, with a few admirable notes in an appendix; Thomas Jackson (Wesleyan minister, *Expos. Disc.*, London, 1839); Dr F. W. Krummacher in his *Sabbath-glocke*, and Dr Wheaton (Hartford, 1850). Also *St Paul and Philemon*, by C. S. Bere (S.P.C.K., 1876).

Larger Pulpit Expositions. — Six Lectures in *Sermons and Miscellaneous Works of Rev. Samuel Knight*, A.M. (Halifax, 1828), *Méditations sur quelques portions de la Parole de Dieu*, par A. Rochat (Paris, 1842): F. Kühne, *Der Epist. Pauli an Phil. in Bibelstunden*, etc. (Leipsic, 1856); Samuel Cox, *Private Letters of St Paul and St John* (London, 1867); six meditations on Philemon, entitled *Grosse Liebe im Kleinen Leben*, by Pastor Quandt, of the Hague (Berlin, 1869); and *Studies on Philemon, Exegetical and Homiletic*, a posthumous volume, by Robert Nisbet, D.D. (Blackwood, Edinburgh and London, 1876). The Exposition and Homiletics in the *Pulpit Commentary* are by Rev. S. J. Eales, D.C.L. (1887). The vol. by Dr Alex. M'Laren of Manchester (in the *Expositor's Bible* Series, Hodder & Stoughton, 1892) on Colossians and Philemon is in the preacher's highest style. A Scottish pulpit contributes on this Epistle, *A Series of Expositions* by A. K. MacMurchy (8vo, 1898).

THE END

1982-83 TITLES

TITLES CURRENTLY AVAILABLE

TITLES CURRENTLY AVAILABLE

4102	Morison, James	The Gospel According to Mark	21.00
4201	Kelly, William	The Gospel of Luke	18.50
4301	Brown, John	The Intercessory Prayer of Our Lord Jesus Christ	11.50
4302	Hengstenberg, E. W.	Commentary on the Gospel of John (2 vol.)	34.95
4401	Alexander, Joseph	Commentary on the Acts of the Apostles (2 vol. in 1)	27.50
4402	Gloag, Paton J.	A Critical and Exegetical Commentary on Acts (2 vol.)	29.95
4403	Stier, Rudolf E.	Words of the Apostles	18.75
4501	Shedd, W. G. T.	Critical and Doctrinal Commentary on Romans	17.00
4502	Moule, H. C. G.	The Epistle to the Romans	16.25
4601	Brown, John	The Resurrection of Life	15.50
4602	Edwards, Thomas C.	A Commentary on the First Epistle to the Corinthians	18.00
4801	Ramsay, William	Historical Commentary on the Epistle to the Galatians	17.75
4802	Brown, John	An Exposition of the Epistle of Paul to the Galatians	16.00
5001	Johnstone, Robert	Lectures on the Book of Philippians	18.25
5102	Westcott, F. B.	The Epistle to the Colossians	7.50
5103	Eadie, John	Colossians	10.50
5401	Liddon, H. P.	The First Epistle to Timothy	6.00
5601	Taylor, Thomas	An Exposition of Titus	20.75
5801	Delitzsch, Franz	Commentary on the Epistle to the Hebrews (2 vol.)	31.50
5802	Bruce, A. B.	The Epistle to the Hebrews	17.25
5901	Johnstone, Robert	Lectures on the Epistle of James	16.50
5902	Mayor, Joseph B.	The Epistle of St. James	20.25
6201	Lias, John J.	The First Epistle of John	15.75
6601	Trench, Richard C.	Commentary on the Epistles to the Seven Churches	8.50
7001	Orelli, Hans C. von	The Twelve Minor Prophets	15.50
7002	Alford, Dean Henry	The Book of Genesis and Part of the Book of Exodus	12.50
7003	Marbury, Edward	Obadiah and Habakkuk	23.95
7004	Adeney, Walter	The Books of Ezra and Nehemiah	13.00
7101	Mayor, Joseph B.	The Epistle of St. Jude and The Second Epistle of Peter	16.50
7102	Lillie, John	Lectures on the First and Second Epistles of Peter	19.75
7103	Hort, F. J. A. & Hort, A. F.	Expository and Exegetical Studies	29.50
7104	Milligan, George	St. Paul's Epistles to the Thessalonians	12.00
7105	Stanley, Arthur P.	Epistles of Paul to the Corinthians	20.95
7106	Moule, H. C. G.	Colossian and Philemon Studies	12.00
7107	Fairbairn, Patrick	The Pastoral Epistles	17.25
8001	Fairweather, William	Background of the Gospels	17.00
8002	Fairweather, William	Background of the Epistles	16.50
8003	Zahn, Theodor	Introduction to the New Testament (3 vol.)	48.00
8004	Bernard, Thomas	The Progress of Doctrine in the New Testament	9.00
8401	Blaikie, William G.	David, King of Israel	17.50
8402	Farrar, F. W.	The Life and Work of St. Paul (2 vol.)	43.95
8601	Shedd, W. G. T.	Dogmatic Theology (4 vol.)	52.50
8602	Shedd, W. G. T.	Theological Essays (2 vol. in 1)	26.00
8603	McIntosh, Hugh	Is Christ Infallible and the Bible True?	27.00
8701	Shedd, W. G. T.	History of Christian Doctrine (2 vol.)	31.50
8703	Kurtz, John Henry	Sacrificial Worship of the Old Testament	16.50
8901	Fawcett, John	Christ Precious to those that Believe	10.00
9401	Neal, Daniel	History of the Puritans (3 vol.)	54.95
9402	Warns, Johannes	Baptism	13.25
9501	Schilder, Klass	The Trilogy (3 vol.)	48.00
9502	Liddon, H. P. & Orr, J.	The Birth of Christ	15.25
9503	Bruce, A. B.	The Parables of Christ	15.50
9504	Bruce, A. B.	The Miracles of Christ	20.00
9505	Milligan, William	The Ascension of Christ	15.00
9506	Moule, H. C. & Orr, J.	The Resurrection of Christ	20.00
9507	Denney, James	The Death of Christ	12.50
9508	Farrar, F. W.	The Life of Christ	24.95
9509	Dalman, Gustaf H.	The Words of Christ	13.50
9510	Andrews, S. & Gifford, E. H.	Man and the Incarnation & The Incarnation (2 vol. in 1)	15.00
9511	Baron, David	Types, Psalms and Prophecies	14.00
9512	Stier, Rudolf E.	Words of the Risen Christ	8.25
9801	Liddon, H. P.	The Divinity of Our Lord	20.50
9802	Pink, Arthur W.	The Antichrist	12.00
9803	Shedd, W. G. T.	The Doctrine of Endless Punishment	8.25
9804	Andrews, S. J.	Christianity and Anti-Christianity in Their Final Conflict	15.00
9805	Gilpin, Richard	Biblical Demonology: A Treatise on Satan's Temptations	20.00